# WILLIAM McKINLEY

# WILLIAM McKINLEY

by EDWIN P. HOYT

REILLY & LEE COMPANY · CHICAGO

ILLUSTRATIONS REPRODUCED THROUGH THE COURTESY
OF THE BETTMANN ARCHIVE, INC.

# Table of Contents

# CHAPTER 1

# Ohio Boyhood

ALTHOUGH THE WORLD will never say that William McKinley was one of the great Presidents of the United States, neither will he be numbered finally among the weakest of them. He was a good President. In many ways he was a strong President. During his term in office the United States faced—and conquered—several pressing and important domestic problems, chiefly the recurrent issues of the currency and basic approach to taxation. A Republican, McKinley was influential in the reform of the civil service, following policies begun by the Republican, James Garfield, and strengthened by the Democrat, Grover Cleveland.

But more important than any domestic issue that arose in McKinley's career as President were a number of matters of international importance. The problem of the Panama Canal came to disturb the nation and invigorate it. The question of imperialism arose—or, rather, became urgent. Imperialism had been a matter of interest and concern since the first Cleveland administration. America's adventure in imperialism was a long time in being formed, yet it could be stated simply that the McKinley administrations represented the high point of American expansionism outside the continental limitations imposed by the original founding fathers.

President McKinley's policies were the result of public pressures, political compromises and principle, as have been those of all occupants of the White House in one way or another. McKinley brought many qualities to the presidency, chief among them a quiet integrity and a quiet bravery which were little known to men and women outside his intimate circle. He faced many problems which had not before troubled the nation, including the rise of radicalism during and after depression years. How he met those problems, and the change in course of the American nation because it was his particular personality that guided the country between 1897 and 1901, are not very well known because McKinley has been overshadowed by Theodore Roosevelt in history. In many ways, however, the policies begun by Theodore Roosevelt in the beginning of his presidency were the result of planning by McKinley and his friend, manager, and political advisor, Mark Hanna.

McKinley was one of the "Ohio Presidents," a group of men who were very prominent in American affairs at the end of the Civil War, most of whom had been officers in the Union ranks. Garfield was one. So were Rutherford B. Hayes and Benjamin Harrison. Partly for its role in the war and partly because of its growing population and key position in industry and transportation, Ohio was the most important state in the Union outside the eastern seaboard, and proudly called itself the home of Presidents.

William McKinley was born with several of the attributes considered in the nineteenth century to be essential for holding the nation's highest office. He was the son of honest but not wealthy parents. He was a Protestant, and white, and he came from the heartland of America. In the beginning this latter quality had not been needed: the

Virginia Presidents were all gentlemen and the Adamses were from the finest New England family stock. But after Andrew Jackson, it seemed almost imperative that a presidential candidate be born in a log cabin. The log cabin disappeared from politics with Benjamin Harrison and Grover Cleveland—the American people were becoming more sophisticated in the 1880's—but the principle of humble birth was retained.

William McKinley's ancestors were Scottish highlanders and they sent a son to America in the eighteenth century. He was David McKinley, sometimes known as David the Weaver because of his trade in the old country. He bought 316 acres of land on the shores of the Susquehanna River in Pennsylvania in 1743. His son John inherited part of that land and worked hard to become an important landholder in the area. He fought in the American Revolution with the York County Militia of Pennsylvania colony. So did his son David, who was born in 1755. David served for 21 months and fought in three engagements before the war ended. He moved west after the war and finally settled in Columbiana County, Ohio. There he settled down to raise a family, having ten children in all, including James Stevenson McKinley, the grandfather of William McKinley.

James married an Englishwoman named Mary Rose, who had been born in Europe and had come to America with her family, as had so many others, to escape religious intolerance in Europe. This, again, was a part of the essential spirit of America and American political leaders; for having courage to escape intolerance indicated a high level of character on the part of Mary Rose—the kind of character often associated with the development of leadership.

James and Mary McKinley moved to a farm, but later James went into the iron business and became manager of a

charcoal furnace at what is now Lisbon, Ohio. There were
many such furnaces in the United States before the Besse-
mer process was discovered to revolutionize the metal industry. Each of these iron furnaces made a small quantity
of pig iron or even flat iron each year, serving its local region, until the iron companies began to consolidate and to
produce the stronger product called steel.

James' son William, father of the President, grew up in
the iron business, chopping trees and splitting them into
firing lengths, burning the wood to make charcoal, and buying or even finding the ore. He grew up, without education
except that of the common school where he learned to read
and write, and went into the iron business on his own. He
rented a furnace at Niles, Ohio, which he operated for a
number of years. In 1829 he married Nancy Allison, another Scottish descendant, and a strong Methodist, who
had little more education than her husband.

William McKinley, Jr., who was to become the twenty-
fifth President of the United States, was the seventh child of
William and Nancy McKinley. Four girls and two boys
were born before him. William was born in Niles, Ohio,
on January 29, 1843, in a wooden cottage—not a log cabin
—on the corner of the main street in the village. Part of the
house was used as a store.

He went to school at Niles. As a boy he played soldier,
wearing a paper hat and carrying a wooden "musket." He
played with great enthusiasm, along with the other boys,
because this was the period of the Mexican War and the
expansion across the West. He went puddling in Mosquito
Creek (where one day he nearly drowned, and would have,
had it not been for a timely rescue by a young man).

In 1852, when young William was nine years old, his
family moved to Poland, a small village in Mahoning

County, Ohio, so the children could better their education. The family moved, but William McKinley, Sr., could not. He must stay near the sources of iron ore to run his furnace, and he did this, going to live with his family only on weekends.

Poland was a prosperous village. It had five stores, a Presbyterian church, a Methodist church, a grist mill, a saw mill, a cotton mill, its own foundry, and about a hundred houses. It also boasted an academy, where William and his brothers went to school. This Poland Seminary had been opened in 1830 to teach the classics and English literature, or at least the tradition of higher education in Poland extended back that far. The academy had actually come into being under B. F. Lee in 1849. When William attended the school, the faculty consisted of four teachers, and even lessons in instrumental music were offered. The three-story building was so impressive that, in the fashion of the growing West, it was called "the college." Here William McKinley went to school.

After seven years at the academy, he entered Allegheny College at Meadville, Pennsylvania. He had scarcely begun his studies at Allegheny, however, when he became ill and had to withdraw for the year and return to Poland. He firmly intended, he said, to go back to Allegheny the next year and start again, but that ambition could not be satisfied. When he was well again, hard times had come to the Western Reserve area of Ohio and it was necessary for him to help support the large family. (Nine children were born in all.)

William did what so many boys had done before when they had the rudiments of education: he found a job teaching in a district school some two miles from Poland. He was paid $25 a month, and he could have boarded with various families but chose to walk back and forth to home instead. He held this post for a year, and then in the summer of 1861 he took a job as a clerk in the post office in Poland.

After the Confederates fired that first shot at Fort Sumter, it took some time for the people of the north to realize that the nation was truly at war. But realize it they did at the Battle of Bull Run, when the southerners routed a highly superior Union force and might have moved swiftly against Washington had they known how disorganized the Union army really was. In June, men from Poland began to enlist in the Union army, and William, who was eighteen, caught the war fever. Poland's first contingent of citizen-soldiers was raised that month, and William and his cousin William Osborne drove to Youngstown to see the company leave for Columbus. In it were many young men they knew well. On the way to Youngstown and back they discussed the idea of enlisting, and when they returned to Poland, William McKinley went to his mother to ask her permission to leave. He did this because he was a proper son, and because he felt some responsibility to the family, as his departure would make it harder on them financially.

So William McKinley enlisted in the service of his country, to become a private in Company E of the Twenty-third Ohio Volunteers. The enlistment was only for three months' time. This was common in the early days of the Civil War. Most people still believed the war would end in a short time; they could not bear to believe otherwise.

But when this particular group came to Columbus, the authorities informed them that the three months' quota was filled, and that they must enlist for three years or go home and wait for the next call. William and his friends enlisted, then, for three years in the United States army on June 11, 1861.

Their commander was William S. Rosecrans, who was to become a famous Union general. The first major was Rutherford B. Hayes, who was to become President of the United States. William McKinley was much impressed with Hayes over one incident which occurred at the beginning of their association. The independent citizen-soldiers of Ohio took one look at the weapons the army issued, and refused them. The soldiers were quite right—the guns were certainly inferior, but they were the only guns available to the Ohio troops at that moment, and Hayes knew it very well. He stood up before the mutinous troops and told them how battles had been won at Bunker Hill and Lexington with inferior weapons. Even that was not the point, he said; those weapons could provide the men the training they needed, and then they would be better able to use the modern guns that were coming. The men listened and believed, and the mutiny ended.

Six weeks after William's enlistment, his regiment was ordered to Clarksburg, Virginia, and then to the little town of Weston, really a village of about eight hundred people. There they guarded bridges, chased skunks they thought erroneously to be Confederates or "seceshers," and sometimes killed livestock in brushes with "the enemy." They were camped in a bend of the Monongahela River. In their free time they bathed in the river, lolled in tents or in the sunshine, and learned the arts of soldiering as quickly as their officers could teach them. Their training was brief, however, for the men were soon committed for action as a part of General Rosecrans' army. In September they began marching through the mountains, and on September 10 they were face to face with the enemy in the engagement at Carnifex Ferry. There the Confederates were forced to retreat after a skirmish. They left some wounded and some prisoners, but the majority of the enemy force made its way safely out of the region controlled by the Union troops under the cover of a fierce rainstorm.

"This was our first real fight," William McKinley said many years later, "and the effect of the victory was of far more consequence to us than the battle itself. It gave us confidence in ourselves and faith in our commander. We learned that we could fight and whip the rebels on their own ground."

After this minor battle, the regiment moved back to Camp Ewing, where it remained for much of the autumn and winter. This camp was badly located. It was on low ground, and the sanitary facilities were poor. Many men came down with illnesses that in those days were simply diagnosed as "fever." There were many losses to the regiment from sickness, far more than had been lost in enemy action. In fact, there was no more enemy action that year. Not until April, 1862, did the Ohio men of McKinley's regiment see action again. On April 22, the Twenty-third Ohio set out for Princeton, which was held by the Confederates. The southerners burned the town and retreated in the face of the attacks. On May 8, nine companies of the regiment were attacked by a larger enemy force, although the Union troops were supported by cavalry. They were driven back, finally, to Flat Top Mountain in a running battle over several days. There the enemy broke off the action. Then action came again on August 15, when the regiment was ordered to march to Camp Platt on the Great Kanawha River. There the troops were embarked after a forced march of 104 miles in three days—through the mountains. They boarded transport steamers and were taken to Parkersburg, then they were taken by train to Washington to join the army of General George McClellan.

McClellan led the Army of the Potomac against Frederick, Maryland, to Middletown, and then to fight the Battle of South Mountain on September 13. Four days later came the great Battle of Antietam, one of the most devastating battles of the Civil War, where more men were killed and wounded than in any other single engagement.

"It was a lovely September day," McKinley wrote later, "an ideal Sunday morning. McClellan's army, with Burnside's corps in front, was passing up the mountain by the national road. General Cox's Ohio Division led Burnside's corps, and the Twenty-third Ohio was in the lead of that division. [Major] Hayes was ordered to take one of the mountain paths and move to the right of the rebels. At nine o'clock the rebel picket was driven back, and on our pushing forward the rebels advanced upon us in strong force. Our regiment was quickly formed in the woods and charged over rocks and broken ground, through deep underbrush, under the heavy fire of the enemy at short range, and, after one of the hottest fights of the war, we drove them out of the woods and into an open field near the hilltop. Another charge was ordered by Hayes. No sooner had he given the word of command than a minie ball from the enemy shattered his left arm above the elbow, crushing the bone to fragments. He called to a soldier to tie his handkerchief above the wound, but turning faint he fell, his men passing beyond him into the fight where he had ordered them."

The Twenty-third Ohio fought well that day. It made three successful charges, but its casualties were high. Half the men of the regiment fell—that is, two hundred men were killed or wounded that day in the Twenty-third Ohio.

William McKinley had been appointed commissary sergeant, and at the Battle of Antietam it was his job to feed the troops. The fight began early in the morning, and the men had little to eat. McKinley was two miles behind the front line with the wagons. He saw stragglers coming back from the fight and put them to work. Soon he was moving forward with two mule teams, bringing rations and barrels of coffee that were hot when he left camp. He drove one team and urged the other on. One team was shot down, but he found two more mules and put them into action. He fought his way, under fire, all the way to the front, and in the afternoon reached the rear of the brigade with the welcome food. It was the first time that a Union force was fed at the front while under fire.

Major Hayes told the story to Governor Tod of Ohio when the Major was returned to Ohio for treatment of his wound. The Governor had the power to promote Ohio soldiers in Ohio regiments, and he ordered William McKinley promoted to second lieutenant as of September 24. McKinley was nineteen years old.

CHAPTER 2

# Soldiering

WILLIAM MCKINLEY was at home in Ohio when he learned of his promotion to the officer corps of the Union army. He returned to duty on December 13, 1862, rejoining the old regiment in its winter camp at the falls of the Great Kanawha River. The troops remained there until the following summer when Hayes, now a colonel, was sent out with two regiments and a section of artillery to track down John Morgan, the raider who, with a handful of cavalrymen, was making life miserable for the Union forces by dashing behind their lines, raiding and burning, and then moving on as swiftly as the winds.

Lt. McKinley and the others were sent through the southern counties of Ohio and Indiana to cut Morgan and his men off from the Confederate lines. They succeeded, and eventually Morgan was forced to surrender.

Then, the Twenty-third Ohio was again inactive for many months. On April 29, 1864, they were moved into action—this time in a raid on the Virginia and Tennessee Railroad, led by General Crook. Lt. McKinley was now an aide to Colonel Hayes, and was First Lieutenant of Company E, the company of Poland men with whom he had joined the ranks. Earlier, an officer had written that Mc-

Kinley promised to be "one of the best." He was proving himself a good soldier.

The campaign that began that spring was the hardest yet faced by the Ohioans. "It was a rough and trying march," McKinley wrote, "over mountains and through deep ravines and dense woods, with snows and rains that would have checked the advance of any but the most determined. Daily we were brought in contact with the enemy. We penetrated a country where guerillas were abundant and where it was not an unusual thing for our own men to be shot from the underbrush—murdered in cold blood."

This travel through the wilderness ended in the Battle of Cloyd's Mountain on May 9. The Twenty-third arrived on the battle scene early in the day, and was held until, around noon, the order to move up was given. The enemy was located in trenches on the crest of the foothills of the mountain, with mountain behind them. The hill was thickly wooded, steep, and hard to climb, and at the base of the hill was a small stream which the Union forces must ford in order to carry out their attack. Worst of all, before the stream was a meadow some five hundred yards wide. To the Union soldiers it threatened sudden death; for that meadow must be crossed, and when the men were crossing they were perfect targets for the defenders, burrowing behind their earthworks above the waving grass, able to fire at will.

The position must be taken, no matter what the cost, and the Twenty-third was selected to take it. The order was given, bayonets were fixed, and the men moved out in double time, running, zig-zagging, ducking, twisting and turning, but always headed for that stream and the comparative safety of the woods below the mountain. They ran, they skirted, they fell. Some rose again and some did not. When the barrage of bullets and artillery shells was finally quiet, most of the Twenty-third were on the other side, across the stream and in the woods. The Confederates tried then to depress their guns to bear on the charging enemy, and the riflemen fired at every motion, every flash of blue in the woods.

All this time not a man in the Twenty-third had fired a shot. Their first task was to cross the meadow under that murderous rain of gunfire, and that task had been accomplished. Now the task was to march up the mountain and charge across the earthworks. The Twenty-third moved on, came to the trenches, charged, and after a fierce scuffle captured the trenches and two pieces of artillery. The major enemy force, however, had already moved back to the crest of the mountain. Now the Twenty-third moved again, against that line, but reinforced this time with other Union troops. At the end of the day, bloody and bone tired, the Twenty-third had captured the heights of Cloyd's Mountain and the battle was over.

There was no more respite for the Twenty-third. On May 18 the force moved against Lynchburg, in the mountainous country of central Virginia. But now the Union was in the Confederate heartland and the southerners had no intention of letting their enemies take this important industrial city and arsenal. Reinforcements were brought up from Richmond and a bloody battle was fought near Lynchburg in a forest so dense that the men said they could not see the light of the sun as they fought. The Union troops were forced to retreat—not just back to trenches or a prepared position on a height, but along the road north, pursued constantly by the enemy.

The Confederates were marching. The men of the Twenty-third and the other units were staggering back, dog tired after fighting and marching for two steady weeks. They moved along the road, so tired that some men fell asleep on the march and others collapsed in the ditches, risking capture by the enemy. The men marched and fought for nine days, in touch with the enemy almost all of that time, with very little sleep and almost no food. Finally, after marching 180 miles, they met a supply train at Big Sewall Mountain on May 27, and, reinforced, they broke off with the enemy and camped. They had marched almost constantly for two months, crossed three ranges of the Allegheny Mountains no less than four times, the Blue Ridge Mountains twice, and on several occasions marched all day and all night without any sleep at all.

On July 1, the Twenty-third Ohio reached Charleston, West Virginia, and was given ten days of rest time in which to bring the force up to strength and recuperate from the gruelling encounter with the Confederates.

The Confederates were making up for their losses to a more powerful Union by a series of stabbing raids which often paralyzed whole regions along the border. General Jubal Early was racing in and out of Maryland and Pennsylvania that summer, and the result of his forays was to spread panic along the border region. So after ten short days the Twenty-third Ohio was pulled back into service and sent by way of Parkersburg to Martinsburg and then to Cabletown, just ten miles from the famous Harper's Ferry. Then General Hayes' brigade—only a brigade—was sent to attack General Early in one of the great Union miscalculations of the war. The brigade was surrounded, but fought its way out of the trap and rejoined the force led by General Crook.

The Union intelligence officers learned that General Early was ordered to move his army to Richmond, and they settled down now for some rest. Then, on Sunday morning, July 24, the men heard the cannon banging away, as they put it. They were used to the sound, for it seemed that the artillery and the cavalry were always in motion, whether there were any rebels around or not, but the sound of the firing this time seemed to increase in volume steadily. Couriers came in from the cavalry, telling the men at head-quarters that the cavalry outposts on the valley road, south of Winchester, were being driven in toward the lines by a large force of Confederates. For some time General Crook could not imagine what was happening. Finally it became clear that Early's plans had been changed, and he was fac-ing that large rebel army.

The Union troops were sent to fight at the little hamlet of Kernstown, four miles south of Winchester. They began to form the line of battle and around noon were ready, with Hayes' brigade on the extreme left of the line, extending east of the road into open fields. They faced a rebel force about three times as large as their own.

The battle opened with firing along the line from the artillery of both sides, with the 20,000 Confederates and their superior cannon having it all over the Union forces, with their 6000 men. The Confederates, with a superior cavalry force, sent the horsemen around the left. They soon routed the smaller Union cavalry unit, and in the open ground out past the road the Confederates threatened to turn the flank of the Union and surround the smaller army.

As this threat became apparent in the heat of battle, the center of the Union line broke, and the burden fell on Hayes' brigade to hold. Lieutenant McKinley was a mem-ber of Hayes' staff, and with the situation developing as it did, it was his job to help turn the men and make an or-derly retreat, rather than face rout or capture.

When the retreat was under way it was discovered that Colonel William Brown and the Thirteenth West Virginia Regiment, which had been held in reserve in an orchard about five hundred yards behind the battle line, was left behind. It had not been informed of the change in the bat-

tle plan. Unless something was done—and fast—the Thirteenth West Virginia would be surrounded, cut off, and
lost.

Colonel Hayes needed action. Lieutenant McKinley was
ready. He mounted his horse, spurred him, and raced off
to the orchard to pass the word, galloping through fire so
thick that when one shell struck directly in front of him,
the men behind could not tell if he was lost because the
horse and rider were enveloped in smoke and dust. Mc-
Kinley made the ride safely, delivered the message in the
comparative safety of the orchard, and the Thirteenth West
Virginia joined the retreat and was saved.

Hayes' brigade retreated all afternoon, held together by
the staff officers who rode along the line encouraging the
dusty, weary men. At dark they came to a battery of Union
artillery, four guns and their caissons, which had been
abandoned by more desperate troops. McKinley asked permission to save them, found volunteers among the Twenty-
third Ohio's tired soldiers, and took the guns.

The battle was a serious setback for General Crook's
force. About a fourth of his men were killed, wounded, or
taken prisoner. So many of the officers of the Twenty-third
Ohio were killed that battlefield promotions were in order.
William McKinley was made captain and placed in charge
of Company G of the regiment. He left the regiment very
shortly, however, to join the staff of General Crook.

From July 20 until September 3 Crook's force was engaged in almost constant contact with the Confederates—
not battle but the wearying skirmish and the wearying
patrol. Both commanders were fencing, seeking position before they engaged the other.

On September 3 there was a night battle at Berryville,
Virginia, in which Captain McKinley participated. Then
came more skirmishing until the morning of September
19, when the Battle of Opequan was joined.

The battle began in the morning. General Crook's force was in reserve at the start, but was sent to the right flank to try to move around the enemy's left. Captain McKinley, staff officer to the General now, was sent with a verbal message to Colonel Duval, telling him to move his troops to the far right, but not telling him where to go. The Colonel was balking, asking for more definite orders. Captain McKinley knew there was no time to wait for them. In the General's name he ordered the Colonel to move up a certain ravine. As it happened, the move was made safely and quickly and turned out all right. It might have been the end of McKinley's career, however, had the Confederates set a trap in this ravine as the Colonel had feared. It was a matter of bravery and good luck for Captain McKinley that he was hero instead of fool that day.

The Battle of Opequan ended in victory for the Union forces. The Confederates moved to Fisher's Hill, protected by the Shenandoah River on one side and Massanutten Mountain on the other. It seemed that General Early was in a safe position to reorganize his forces. But it only seemed that way, because on July 22 General Crook led the Union forces across the mountain and attacked the Confederates in the rear with such vigor that the lines broke and Early's army for a time became a mob, running to escape, with General Phil Sheridan's cavalry chasing fast behind.

Early was down, but far from out. For a month he remained clear of the Union forces, bringing up supplies and reinforcements to rebuild his army.

General Sheridan, who was in charge of the army, was called to Washington for meetings and had gone. In charge of the force was Major General Horatio Wright of the Sixth Corps, with headquarters on the north side of Cedar Creek, twenty miles south of Winchester.

General Crook's forces, to which Captain McKinley was assigned, were in a position almost parallel with the Confederate lines. Union intelligence reports indicated that all was quiet along the front, and that there was no move afoot.

The Union intelligence reports were absolutely wrong. On the night of October 18, the weather turned chill and foggy. Pickets on the Union side could scarcely see the fires of the enemy this night. General Early had been making ready for an attack for some time, and now he saw that his chance to surprise the Union forces was great. As night fell, to more completely mask the fogbound land, General Early sent his left flank out to the edge of the Union right flank, and his right flank was taken around the Union army, across the North Fork of the Shenandoah River, to a position in the rear of General Crook.

All this was accomplished in darkness. As dawn's rays fingered through the fog at 4:30, though it was not yet light, the Confederates attacked, filling the air around the Union camp with wild rebel yells. The surprise was complete. Many Union troops were sleeping, and when they were assembled the organization was weak and the attacking rebels began driving the Union back.

General Crook's force was now nearly surrounded, and from every side came the sound of rifle and musket shots. Several officers were killed, and General Hayes had a horse shot from under him.

It seemed that the battle must end in rout or capture of at least Crook's 4000 men, but help was on the way. The help came in the form of General Phil Sheridan, who had set out from Winchester in the morning for headquarters when he heard the cannon begin to speak. He headed for Cedar Creek, expecting a battle.

As Sheridan rode toward the camp he saw the number of stragglers on the road and realized that the battle must be going badly. At Newtown the rout was so complete that Sheridan could not get through the village. The streets were jammed with milling soldiers whose one aim was to try to escape capture by running north, away from the enemy. Sheridan went around the town, and on his detour he met Captain McKinley. When McKinley saw his commander he rode back through the confusion, telling the stragglers to turn, that Sheridan was there to lead them to victory. The men did turn, the units were reformed, and the defeat that seemed imperative in the morning was turned to victory in the afternoon.

Captain McKinley's service was not forgotten. On March 13, 1865, he was promoted to the rank of brevet major (or temporary major) of volunteers. The commission came from President Lincoln on the recommendation of General Crook, approved by General Sheridan. So when the war ended that spring, at twenty-two William McKinley was a major in the Union army, with a record of distinguished and valuable service to his country. He liked military service and might have remained in it; but after the war ended, it soon became obvious that there was little opportunity for men in the professional army. Men who had served as colonels went out to the West to fight Indians as lieutenants and less.

So on July 26, 1865, William McKinley was mustered out of the Union army and left, along with thousands of other young men, to decide what he would do with his life. All the excitement of the last four years made him restless and confused about the future, for at twenty-two, having fought through several major battles, having made major decisions of staff and command, he was again to start all over in a new career.

# CHAPTER 3

# The Young Lawyer

UNLIKE MANY of the young men who had come out of the Union service, William McKinley had a taste for public service. Others sought ways in which they might quickly earn their fortunes; and, indeed, there was much opportunity, both honest and dishonest, in the aftermath of the war. The honest opportunity lay in the growth of new industries. As the railroads spread across the nation they created markets for new and more industrial goods; and as the steel and building industries progressed in the East, better methods were found to produce those goods in this country. That was the legal and proper opportunity that opened for the young men of the Union.

The illegal and improper opportunity involved the exploitation of the victory over the broken South. Thousands of unscrupulous Americans moved south as carpetbaggers, to make their fortunes in the ruins of the home of their former enemies. They exploited the South and ruined the southern economy, some becoming wealthy in the process.

William McKinley did not choose either of these roads. He decided to study law. The manner of study for many years had been to enter the law office of some practicing attorney as a clerk and to study there. Yet there was a new trend. Certain schools had been established for the teaching of the law. After a year of clerking and studying in the office of Judge Charles E. Glidden of Mahoning County, McKinley went to Albany, New York, to enter the Albany Law School. He studied there for most of one year, but in the spring of 1867 felt that he knew enough and that it was time for him to begin earning money. He left the school and went back to Ohio to seek admission to the bar. He was admitted on the motion of Frances E. Hutchins, a lawyer friend, and he moved to the town of Canton, the county seat of Stark County, where his sister Anna was teaching school. Canton was a large place compared to Poland, and the opportunity for a young lawyer was much greater there.

Lawyer McKinley rented an office in a building not far from Market Street, and began to cultivate friends and wait for what luck would bring him. He came to the attention of Judge George W. Belden, one of the most prominent lawyers in Canton, who had offices in the same building. Belden offered him his first opportunity. He handed McKinley some papers one day and asked him to prepare the case outlined for trial the following day. McKinley had never tried a case, and he said he did not know anything about it. Belden encouraged him, and McKinley did try the case and won it. Belden gave him $25 of the $100 fee he had received; but more important, he came to the trial, saw how the young lawyer comported himself, and offered McKinley a partnership. So William McKinley's fortune was assured, by the luck of being in the same office building with a busy lawyer at the right time. Luck alone would never have been enough, of course. McKinley took his chance, when he accepted a court case without preparation or experience. He sat up all night preparing that case. So luck was accompanied by hard work. But luck was there, and for the second time McKinley was wise enough to grasp it by the hand and devote his best efforts to the chance.

McKinley, however, had noticed something about the man's limp that did not seem quite to fit with the case presented by his opponent. He rose to cross examine and asked the poor man to show his other leg. It was even more crooked than the one the surgeon had set.

"My client seems to have done better by this man than nature itself did," he said to the jury, "and I move that the suit be dismissed, with a recommendation to the plaintiff that he have the other leg broken and then set by the surgeon who set the first one."

McKinley became interested in political affairs almost as soon as he began to practice law. His first efforts were connected with the campaign of 1867, when his old commander and friend, Rutherford B. Hayes, was running for governor on the Republican ticket. The Democrats of Ohio were out to return to the old ways, and in Ohio this meant southern ways; for southern Ohio has many of the attributes of the South, and in this period there were many who sympathized with the southerners and who had no use for Negro suffrage.

"We have come here . . . to release the State from the thralldom of Niggerism, and place it under the control of the Democratic party," announced the temporary chairman of the Democratic state convention when it met that year. The Republicans came out for universal suffrage and Negro rights, a position not at all favored in the southern part of the state. The proof of it was in an amendment offered to the state constitution which would promise impartial male suffrage in the state.

McKinley spoke for this amendment at stump meetings around Ohio. He faced a hostile audience at his first speech, which was delivered in the town of New Berlin.

When he came to town, McKinley went to the appointed place, the steps of the village tavern. He was not supposed

to be speaking at all, but one of the speakers of the day had
not appeared and he was asked if he could make a speech.
Now he had some experience in appearing in court, and he
was not afraid. He stepped up on a big box and began; and
although his audience did not like his ideas, they listened
with growing respect because McKinley was a strong
speaker.

He was embarked on a public career then, because travel-
ling and speaking seemed made for his personality. He was
so effective that soon he was called into service by other
political aspirants to work for them.

In the spring of 1869 political ambition began to stir in
William McKinley. He was nominated by the Republican
party to be prosecuting attorney for Stark County. The
county was heavily Democratic in sentiment and it seemed
that the political leaders of the county were simply reward-
ing a good party worker for his speechmaking and organization work. McKinley did not look at it that way at all. He
set out to get himself elected, and succeeded. At the age of
twenty-six he was a political whirlwind, having captured
an office from the political enemy which the Republicans
had never expected to have, and doing it without very much
help from anyone except himself.

The public prosecutor's job was a very good one for a
young politician because it gave him an opportunity to
fight crime. It also afforded an opportunity to meet everyone in the county, and to dispense mercy with justice where
mercy seemed in order. William McKinley was also an able
and honest prosecutor, where many times before small town
prosecutors had been sloppy in performance of their duties.
He took the office seriously, and in 1871 he was renomi-
nated by the Republicans. This time he had party support,
but he also had strong opposition from the Democrats, and

he lost to the same man he had beaten before, William A. Lynch, who happened also to be a close personal friend.

Political defeat certainly did not hurt McKinley in Canton. No one had expected him to win that first election. Now he was far better known than before, and the rigors of the prosecutor's office had instructed him well in the practice of the law. He became a more prominent attorney than before, and was regarded among the socialites of Canton as one of the eminently eligible bachelors.

In 1870 McKinley met Ida Saxton, daughter of one of Canton's most substantial citizens and the town's leading banker besides. Ida Saxton had just returned from the tour of Europe, which marked the young American gentlewoman's emergence into society after her school days. McKinley had been in Canton three years then, and although he was only twenty-seven he was known respectfully as the Major. Saxton took a liking to him and invited him to the house, where he met Ida. There followed a round of picnics, outings, teas, dinners, and a long drive in the country where McKinley asked Ida to marry him. She said she would. They were married on January 25, 1871, in Canton's First Presbyterian Church.

For a time the young couple lived at the St. Cloud Hotel. Then the bride's father gave them a house on North Market Street, and they settled down to make that their permanent home. On Christmas day, 1871, their first child was born, Katharine. In April, 1873, little Ida was born. Neither child lived to adulthood, and from the date of the birth of the second girl, Ida McKinley was a semi-invalid. This was the great tragedy of William McKinley's private life, but it also may have driven him on to his great achievements as a political leader.

CHAPTER 4

# Politician

UNTIL 1875, William McKinley's taste of political life had been very slight. He was really a political amateur, and he was so regarded during the early years by the well-organized Republican machine politicians of Ohio who ruled so vigorously for so long from Columbus.

That year Ohio was stirred by an important national issue which was to affect William McKinley's entire political career. On January 14, 1875, President Ulysses S. Grant approved a law which provided for payment of government debts in specie—which meant metal money. Until that time debts could be paid in paper money, or greenbacks. The Democrats attacked this policy; they wanted the paper money kept in circulation since it was easy to come by, where metal money was not. The Democrats were afraid that a "hard money" policy would keep the banks from lending money freely, that industry could not expand, and that hard times would come in the wake of the hard money. Governor Rutherford Hayes was a candidate for Ohio governor for the third time, and currency was the basic issue on which his campaign was fought; for although it was a national issue, it affected the lives of every Ohioan directly. McKinley made himself known to Republicans and others throughout the entire state that year, joining the list of speakers who carried the Republican hopes and acquitting himself very well. He spoke fervently against the Democratic paper money cause.

Again fortune favored McKinley. Although the vote at the Ohio polls was extremely heavy, the plurality by which Rutherford Hayes was elected was very small, and Hayes and the other political leaders were very much conscious of the men who had worked hard during the campaign to assure this slender victory.

Then came another turn of fate, offering what at first appeared to be a ticket to disaster.

In the spring of 1876 the coal miners of the Tuscarawas Valley of Ohio struck against the coal operators. The operators hired strikebreakers and tried to put an end to the strike. Mark Hanna was a partner in a firm that brought strikebreakers to a mine in Stark County. A gang of these strikebreakers arrived at the mine just as the strikers were holding a meeting. There was a fight, in which George Warmington, Hanna's partner, was nearly killed. The strike erupted in open industrial warfare. The sheriff was called out to restore order, and when he could not, a company of state militia was brought in. Peace came then, but not before the strikers had set fire to the mine and burned the buildings.

Many miners were arrested for this damage and were taken to Canton for trial. At first they could not find any lawyer who would represent them against their employers. Feeling was running high in this conservative community, particularly among the respectable businessmen, and the strikers were regarded as scum.

McKinley was asked to look into this matter because he had a reputation as a fair man. He did so, and discovered that many of the strikers were unjustly accused and had not been involved in the damage. He undertook their defense, unpopular though it was. He managed to secure acquittal of nearly all the men, and then would not take a fee because he knew they had no money, or at least that not all of them were able to help pay the costs. It is also most likely that McKinley's growing political ambition told him that in this case was an opportunity to appeal to a very broad segment of the people, the working class. If he ran for office, he could count on much of the support of the upper class in his district, which included the counties of Carroll, Columbiana, Mahoning, and Stark. The miners' strike and his spirited defense gave him a new opening in politics. So in 1876 McKinley entered a large field of candidates for the Republican nomination to the U.S. House of Representatives.

Politics had changed much in the few years since the end of the Civil War. Earlier, when a man announced his candidacy for a public office, he let it be known that he had been persuaded by his friends and constituents to make the race. It would have seemed crude to him to announce that he had political ambitions. Not so with William McKinley. No one asked him to run, unless his wife did. He was ambitious to become a United States congressman and he said as much.

There were three other candidates, including L. D. Woodworth, the incumbent, a prominent Canton judge and the editor of the Canton *Repository*. McKinley beat them all, carrying every township except one, and he was nominated on the first ballot at the Republican convention of 1876. His district was safely Republican, and in the election in the autumn he won the seat against the Democratic candidate by a majority of 3300 votes. At thirty-three years of age, he was on the threshhold of a public career.

The Forty-fifth Congress, in which William McKinley now sat, was deeply concerned with the problems of taxation. The issue was whether to use taxation, especially duties on imported goods, only as a means of raising money for the support of the federal government, or as a method of protecting the infant American industries from their grown-up counterparts abroad. The question was very serious. Indeed, it was the major issue in the election of 1876 for the presidency, except for the dying issue of the Civil War. This would be the last election in which "the bloody flag of the rebellion" would be waved by the Republicans to defeat the Democrats. In this election, in fact, the bloody flag waved very poorly. The Democrats almost certainly would have won had there not been corruption in the balloting and counting on both sides. The election eventually went to the House of Representatives, where a compromise put Rutherford B. Hayes into the presidency over Samuel J. Tilden.

The tariff occupied a major place in both Republican and Democratic party programs in Congress in 1876. In the session before McKinley was elected, the Republicans had this to say:

"The revenue necessary for current expenditures and the obligations of the public debt must be largely derived from duties upon importations, which, so far as possible, should be adjusted to promote the interests of American labor and advance the prosperity of the whole country."

The Republicans, in other words, stood for a tariff that would protect American business and labor from the cheaper foreign labor. (There was something faintly odorous about the Republican insistence that the interests of "labor" were being protected, when actually the interests of business here were paramount, but that was a typical pronouncement of the times.)

The Democratic position was just the opposite:

"We denounce the present Tariff, levied upon nearly

four thousand articles, as masterpieces of injustice, inequal-
ity, and false pretense. . . . It has impoverished many industries to subsidize a few. . . . It promotes fraud, fosters
smuggling, enriches dishonest officials, and bankrupts
honest merchants. We demand that all customhouse taxation shall be only for revenue."

The Democratic position, in other words, was that free
trade should be fostered. (The Democratic position was
slightly odorous because the Democrats made many false
statements about the tariff system, including the expansion
of the tariff schedule from covering the 1200 articles it
actually covered to "over 4000.")

The intemperance shown by both sides was typical of the
day and indicative of the high emotional level of the campaign for and against the tariff. In Congress the tariff became the greatest "pork barrel" issue of the period, referring to a term that grew up to describe the efforts of congressmen to secure special consideration for their districts.
Each congressman voted on the tariff question according to
the economic interests of the area he represented. Whether
Republican or Democrat, if he came from an industrial
area, he was for a high tariff, levelled for protection of that
particular industry or group of industries which was located
in his district. He did not give a fig for other industries or
for agriculture, but in order to protect his own district's interest he would join other representatives of industrial or
agricultural regions to make up a list of the items to be
protected.

Only those representatives from areas which produced
goods or agricultural products *for which there was no effective foreign competition* favored free trade. For these regions, free trade meant a distinct advantage in pricing—
because when the United States put a tariff on the goods
imported from other lands (such as steel railroad rails), the

foreign lands, such as England, put a tariff on American products such as wool and cotton. There was no statesmanship in it, only continual bickering over the most narrow interests, as viewed most narrowly from the halls of Congress.

When William McKinley came to Congress, he was advised by the new President, Rutherford B. Hayes, that the tariff would be for many years the most important issue in the land, and that he ought to try to make it his special province. He did just that, and before he was finished he made himself the most accomplished Republican advocate of a high tariff (which was quite to be expected, considering the district from which he came). McKinley's position from the beginning was that "self-preservation is the first law of nature, as it is and should be of nations." He believed that self-preservation meant using the tariff to protect an industry in America against its counterpart in other countries. It was a very simple philosophy. Over the years it has been made more complicated than it ought to be by the use of much bombast and many high flown phrases, such as McKinley's own statement of principle:

"It is our duty," he said, "and we ought to protect as sacredly and assuredly the labor and industry of the United States as we would protect her honor from taint or her territory from invasion."

Yet with William McKinley this attitude was not a pose. He was not a faker or a political opportunist. He believed what he said. These strong and knightly words came from a man of fervent patriotism. His feelings led him to establish the most aggressive foreign policy the United States had ever known until his presidency. His first encounters with national public problems, in the matter of the tariff, pointed the way that William McKinley would lead the country when he came to power.

The McKinley who took his seat in the House of Representatives when the Forty-fifth Congress convened was an
impressive figure, handsome and well dressed in the style of
the period. He wore a conservative long-tailed dark coat
with wide, sharp-pointed lapels, high button black shoes,
trousers to match the coat but without regard to crease in
the front, a stiff white shirt with studs and a detachable collar, heavy cufflinks, and a large flat black bow tie. His face
was rectangular and regular, a little heavier at the jowl than
might be considered handsome in the middle of the twentieth century; but in the nineteenth century there was no
disgrace in plumpness. It was rather highly regarded as sign
of solidity in both men and women. His mouth was firm,
and his face was saved from too much regularity by a deep
cleft dimple in his chin. His eyes were deep set and probing,
beneath beetling brows. His hair was brown, a little thin
and receding from his forehead. All this gave him a dignity
he needed, because he was entering Congress with no previous legislative experience and he needed every assistance
he could get from his appearance and personality.

In the Forty-fifth Congress no young Republican could
hope to rise to any great heights as a public figure. The
Congress was split, and the House of Representatives was
comfortably controlled by the Democrats, which meant
they would organize the House and maintain chairman-
ships of all committees. Fortunately for tempers all around,
the matter of the election of the President had been handled
by the outgoing Forty-fourth Congress in the spring of
1877. The Forty-fifth Congress, although elected in the
fall of 1876, would not begin to sit until December of 1877,
as was the custom in America until the Twentieth Amendment was added to the Constitution in 1933.

Ordinarily, then, the newly elected congressman had
nothing to do for more than a year after his victory. But in

1877 this was not the case; for in order to consider a number of serious problems, the Forty-fifth Congress was called into special session by President Hayes in October, 1877. One problem was that of the currency.

When Congress met, it voted to resume coinage of silver dollars. This was not exactly what Hayes had wanted, and he vetoed the bill. It was passed over his veto, with Congressman McKinley, a Republican from Ohio and nominally a supporter of Hayes, supporting the silver measure against his President.

McKinley's first public effort in the House of Representatives was to present a petition from the iron manufacturers in his district, calling on Congress to refrain from tampering with the tariff laws until it had conducted an investigation into the needs of the country. This was an eminently sane idea, and could not be opposed by any fair person. McKinley received some recognition among Democrats and Republicans for offering so reasonable a proposal.

His first speech on tariff matters came in April of the following year, after he had put in many hours in the library and in his office studying taxation and government finance. He made a very strong and impressive speech against tampering with the tariff. (The Democrats, who were in control of the House, wished to eliminate some of the protective features of the tariff.) This particular speech was to cost McKinley dearly in years to come, perhaps because it was so effective. It may not have made any difference, as it turned out, that he spoke so strongly for the protective tariff.

What happened was this. In 1878 the Democrats secured control of the Ohio state legislature and decided to try to unseat William McKinley by a process, then very popular, known as gerrymandering.

In 1812, when Elbridge Gerry was governor of Massachusetts, his party (the Republicans of the earlier Jefferson days) decided to redistrict the state, to make it easier to maintain political control. They arranged the districts in a strange fashion. Later, a newspaper editor marked out the lines of his district in color on a map and hung it in his office. One day Gilbert Stuart, the portrait painter, visited the office and looked at the map. He picked up a pencil, added wings, claws, and a head, and said that would do for a salamander (referring to a mythical winged beast, not the little animal we know). "Better call it a Gerry-mander," said the editor. The story was widely circulated by the Federalists as a gibe against the Republicans. It may not have been true (there is another tale, involving the same facts but different people), but it is certainly true that the redistricting occurred under Governor Gerry, and that he received the credit for the political maneuver.

When the Democrats went to Columbus after the election, they turned the state's political map upside down. McKinley's district consisted of Stark County, where he lived, Mahoning, where he had been brought up, Columbiana and Carroll. The Democrats removed the last three counties, where McKinley was popular, and placed Asbland, Wayne, and Poetage counties in the district with Stark County. The result, in the election of 1878, was that McKinley's majority was *increased* from 3300 to 3571. The Democrats had made a few miscalculations. They had expected to win with their candidate, General Aquila Wiley, by some 2500 votes.

So a laughing William McKinley returned to Washington in the autumn of 1878. In his first season in office, McKinley had been given a seat on the relatively unimportant committee on the revision of federal laws. He made his reputation from the beginning not as committeeman, but for his forthright support of measures dear to the hearts of

the Republican party. When Congress resumed session in
1878, McKinley came out strongly against a move to repeal
certain laws that protected the currency. He was a strong
advocate of hard metal money, as opposed to paper money,
and he followed this course consistently.

In this period McKinley joined Garfield and others who
were very definitely in the radical Republican camp. He
felt very strongly that the South should be punished for its
rebellion. McKinley was not ready to give the former
enemies of his youth full freedom. When a bill was presented which would enable former Confederate officers to
be returned to the United States army, he opposed it. It
was too soon, he said. He also felt that the Negroes must be
guaranteed the right to vote. As it turned out, the compromise of 1876 allowed the southerners to disenfranchise the
Negroes. The Ku Klux Klan rode high, and even after it
was officially disbanded it managed to keep the Negroes
from becoming full-fledged citizens. Since Congress was
controlled by the Democrats, President Hayes found it very
difficult to protect any of the results of the northern victory after 1878. The Democrats used the system of attach-
ing riders to bills in order to enforce their wishes. They
chose the most important bills of all, the appropriations
bills. If no money was appropriated by Congress to run the
federal administration, the federal government must fall.
So congressmen who detested the Democratic ideas were
sometimes pushed into voting for them. James Garfield led
the fight in Congress against the riders that would put
power totally in the hands of the whites. He was assisted by
William McKinley, who spoke against these measures on
April 18, 1879. He made serious charges.

The attempt was endangering the Constitution, he said.
It would destroy the veto power of the President, one of
the checks provided for the orderly working of the Ameri-

can government. "It in effect says you dare not exercise your veto prerogative even though you do not approve of our legislation; if you do, the wheels of the government must stop." This, he said, overrode one of the constitutional guarantees, that of freedom of action of the executive branch. "It is the first step in the pathway of revolution," McKinley said.

In 1880 McKinley's fortunes rose higher among Ohio Republicans. The Republicans had won control of the legislature again, and the results of Democratic gerrymandering were wiped out, and the old districts were recreated. There was a new problem this year, however. There had been a popular feeling in Ohio that two terms was enough for any representative, and while this was not always honored in observance, it did provide an argument for ambitious men who wished to go to Congress. From every one of William McKinley's four counties came a candidate to oppose him at the state convention. McKinley was shrewd, and fortunate, enough to be appointed temporary chairman of the Ohio State Republican convention that year. The honor was great, but the responsibility was not. The temporary chairman's role was to make an opening address—set the keynote for the convention, in a sense—and then hold office only for the very short period during which the permanent chairman was elected. This man was the real power in the convention.

Holding the temporary chairmanship, however, put McKinley squarely in the eye of the convention. To have denied him return to his own seat would, in a sense, have been to repudiate the keynote of the convention and all that Ohio Republicans said they stood for. It was a very neat political trick, and it got him out of the box into which the rise of so many opponents had placed him.

The year 1880 was an important year for all Ohio Republicans. James G. Blaine was desperate for the Republican presidential nomination, but it went to Ohio's James A. Garfield. This put William McKinley in a key national position, for he was Garfield's right hand man in the House on several issues. In the fall of 1880 and the spring of 1881 the name of William McKinley rose quickly to the top of the list of congressional leaders.

His position worsened considerably after the assassination of Garfield—not because Arthur was particularly unfriendly to him, but because he no longer had that intimacy at the White House that could be so valuable to a congressman. That was why he had so much difficulty in the 1882 Ohio elections. Again he faced the old complaint of having been too long in office. The struggle within the Republican party caused some ill feeling.

McKinley's difficulty became far more serious because Ohio went heavily Democratic that year and elected thirteen of the Democratic candidates for Congress out of a total of twenty-one seats. In McKinley's district the contest was very close. At the end of it, he claimed victory by *eight* votes and went to Washington to take his seat. He was one of only seven Republicans elected to the Ohio congressional delegation.

But McKinley was not to remain long in that delegation. He might have held his seat if the Congress had been in Republican hands, but it was dominated by the Democrats, and when Jonathan H. Wallace, McKinley's Democratic opponent, came to protest, he was awarded the seat by the House in a party struggle.

McKinley was again a private citizen, then, with an open future. He could do as so many unseated congressmen had done and seek an appointed position in the Republican administration. Or he could settle down in Washington to practice law as others had done before him, becoming a

lobbyist or corporation counsel. Not McKinley. He went
home to Canton and prepared to fight for the nomination
in 1884.

But before the 1884 congressional elections the Democrats, who controlled the Ohio legislature, again gerrymandered McKinley's district. They attached Stark County
to Wayne County on the west and Summit and Medina
counties on the northwest, fully expecting thus to maintain a Democratic majority of about 900 votes in the congressional district. McKinley campaigned hard in 1884,
and the Democratic majority disappeared, to become a majority of votes for McKinley of some 2000.

For the next six years he was safe, because the Republicans came back into control of Ohio politics and the gerry-
mander was once more turned back to the original district.
In 1888, for example, McKinley won over his Democratic
opponent by 4100 votes.

In Congress, McKinley became very prominent. He
sought the speakership of the House in 1889, running
against Thomas B. Reed, Joseph G. Cannon, and David B.
Henderson. Reed won, but this did not diminish McKinley
in the eyes of his associates. He was made Republican leader
in the House, and became a member of the House Rules
committee at a time when it was drafting an important new
set of rules for that governing body. He also became chairman of the Committee on Ways and Means, which meant
he was the responsible member of Congress at a time when
that committee was drafting a new tariff bill. In this position he framed the law for which he would become a hero to
the Republicans and anathema to the Democrats: the new
tariff measure, known as the McKinley Tariff. It had come
about because of the strange situation in which the American government found itself in the 1880's.

In those years the Democrats seemed to be proved right.

The country had suffered a terrible depression beginning with the Panic of 1873, and it was very slow in coming out from under the effects of this depression. President Grover Cleveland, the first President since the Civil War to disregard that conflict in his management of the presidency, had held that most of America's troubles could be laid to the huge government surplus that was piling up every year in Washington. He made his campaign on this issue in 1888, although all the responsible leaders of his party said it was suicidal to go against the popular feeling which favored a protective tariff. The issue now went across party lines, and there were many Democrats who deserted Cleveland in 1888 because of it.

Benjamin Harrison of Indiana was elected President on a program of maintenance of the high protective tariff. Almost immediately, however, it became apparent that Cleveland had been right in blaming America's economic problems on the high tariff. Here is what was happening:

The federal government was spending about three hundred million dollars a year then for government operations. Even with the high protective tariff, Americans were buying enough from foreign firms to run the government revenues up to ninety million dollars a year, and then up to more than one hundred and twenty-five million, with no end in sight. Every time the government surplus of money increased, more money went into the Treasury and was thus unavailable—to banks to loan to businessmen, or for anyone to spend in any way. The government could not get rid of its surplus money except by spending, and it could not spend enough money to make up the difference between revenues and expenses deemed necessary.

The government began buying back all the bonds it had issued. But people had bought those bonds for investment and they did not want to give them up. What could they do with the money that would be as safe as having it in government bonds? They wanted more bonds available, not fewer. It became apparent to the Republicans that they would have to lower the protective tariff, no matter how strongly they had defended it. The government was in trouble. President Harrison saw this, and when he was inaugurated in 1889 he promised a change.

The job of planning the change was given to the House Committee on Ways and Means, and thus put in the hands of William McKinley.

In the spring of 1890 McKinley and his fellow committee members prepared the McKinley Tariff Bill. Every industrial representative in the nation was heard by the committee, if he wished to be. The committee's aim was to cut back revenue from certain items, but to retain the protective feature of the bill. There was only one way to do this: to give subsidies to certain American industries if the tariff was to be reduced. That way, Congress took the money out of the hands of the Treasury and put it in the hands of the American businessmen.

The matter of sugar illustrates how it was done. In 1889 sugar and molasses brought in $55,975,610 in revenue. Sugar and molasses were then put on the "free list," which meant no more duties were to be paid on them when these products were imported. But the producers of American sugar, in Louisiana and Texas and elsewhere, could not compete with the cheaper imported sugar. This was solved by paying a "bounty," or subsidy, of two cents a pound to American sugar producers who made sugar from cane, beets, or sorghum that was produced inside the United States. Here was the first major government subsidy of a general agricultural product except in time of war or other emergency. Even the Republicans were afraid of the idea, but it did promise to put an end to that frightening government surplus which kept building up year after year. The people had cheap sugar. The American producers were given a two-cent-a-pound margin of safety so they knew their sugar could be sold.

Other changes were made. The committee proposed an increase of a cent a pound on the wool duty, which would— or was supposed to—stimulate the amount of wool grown domestically. They also planned to increase the protective duty on tin plate, which was sheet iron or steel coated with tin and used for many purposes, including the manufacture of cans for canned goods.

There was some rather high feeling in America on the subject of tin plate. In 1873 some American companies had decided to go into the tin plate business. Across the sea, in Wales, where much tin was produced from mines that had existed since the days of Caesar, the manufacturers met this threat with a price cut. The price of tin fell from $12 a box unit to $4.50 a box. The American mills were forced out of business, and then the price was jumped to $10 a box again —not quite as high as before, just to keep out competition. The Welsh manufacturers then had a monopoly; and when the United States government put a high tariff on tin, the tariff was simply added onto the price and the American consumers paid it.

McKinley proposed a jump in the tariff rate from one cent a pound to 2.2 cents a pound, or an increase of 120 percent. He wanted to encourage the American manufacture of tin plate, which could be carried out in mills in Ohio as well as anywhere else. One thing can be said: McKinley did establish the tin plate industry in America, although his law was changed greatly in later years.

On May 21, 1890, the McKinley Tariff was passed in the House of Representatives. The voting was almost entirely along party lines—164 in favor (all Republicans), 142

against (140 Democrats, one Independent, and one Republican). Six Republicans and fifteen Democrats did not vote
at all on the issue. A similar bill was passed by the Senate,
and after some revision it was passed in a conference committee of both houses and was signed by President Harrison on October 1.

And what happened then?

The public became frightened half to death.

Merchants and manufacturers used the new tariff as an
excuse for raising prices on hundreds of manufactured
items. The price of tin-plate coffeepots jumped from about
$.50 to $1.50. Tin coffee cups went up five times, to a quar-
ter of a dollar. The American surplus began to shrink, and
fear was in the air.

In Ohio, Representative McKinley was again standing
for reelection. The Democrats had come back into control
and again gerrymandered the district. McKinley was running in a district where, the year before, the Democrats had
won by 2900 votes in the state and local elections.

McKinley campaigned very hard, talking on street cor-
ners and at public meetings. He could sense the people's
feeling against his tariff, but he was convinced that he was
right and he stuck to it. On election night he was at Republican headquarters when the news came in: he had been defeated, and so had many other advocates of the high protective tariff. Even though his defeat was by only 300 votes, it
was as decisive as if it had been 3000, or 30,000. Again he
was reduced to private citizen—he who had been the second
most powerful Republican in the House of Representatives.

# CHAPTER 5

# Years of Decision

FOLLOWING HIS DEFEAT for the House of Representatives, William McKinley took time out to reappraise his situation. He had been extremely active in Republican politics in Ohio, attending the national conventions of his party as a delegate since 1884. In this connection he had become friendly with a Cleveland industrialist, Marcus A. Hanna, who owned the Cleveland *Herald* and was very strong in Republican party politics. In 1884 McKinley had handled the delicate problem of resolutions before the National Republican Convention, as chairman of the resolutions committee, which drew up the platform of the party. He made himself known as a strong figure that year in an entirely unofficial manner, too.

One day during the convention when the committee on rules had presented its business, the delegates got into a hot argument over the manner in which the next convention's delegates would be chosen. This was always a serious issue. Two reports were made, and the debate started on a high plane. But it finished in a series of little arguments, with men standing up all around the arena shouting at one another.

General John B. Henderson of Missouri, the permanent chairman of the convention, was an elderly man, and he could not make himself heard above the confusion and the babble. The problem was compounded by emotion: one manner of handling the selection of delegates would disappoint many Negroes, and some twenty of them were on the floor shouting. Twice as many white men were on the floor shouting back, and it looked as if some unpleasantness might develop. The chairman pounded his gavel, but the convention was out of control.

Into this breach stepped William McKinley. He took the gavel, pounded it once sharply. Shouting in his best Union army major's voice, he demanded that the convention come to order. The convention did come to order.

McKinley distinguished himself in other ways at that convention, and at subsequent state conventions of the Republican party. By 1888, when he attended the Republican National Convention as a delegate, he had attracted enough attention that he received one unwanted vote for President when the nominations became deadlocked—and then another, until finally he had eight of them. McKinley and the Ohio delegation had come to the convention to support John Sherman of Ohio. Were McKinley to try to attract votes for himself, it was uncertain whether he would succeed; he might, because the convention always was subject to stampede. But if he failed, he would lose his influence in Ohio as a man who could be trusted.

McKinley arose when the third ballot had brought him those unwanted eight votes and demanded that his name be withdrawn.

At this convention of 1888, McKinley and Mark Hanna became stout friends. Hanna sensed that McKinley had a powerful future ahead of him in politics, and he was looking for a man whom he could boost into the presidency. Hanna had what it took to help boost a man, too. Not only was he a multi-millionaire, but he also was a marvelous

organizer in business and politics. He already favored the
author of the high protective tariff that worked to Hanna's
advantage as a manufacturer. Further, McKinley had
aroused Hanna's interest by refusing the nomination. He
admired the way McKinley had told the convention, "I do
not request—I demand, that no delegate who would not
cast reflection upon me shall cast a ballot for me." Hanna
favored McKinley for still another reason: he was certain
that with McKinley the Republicans could win an election,
and he was very eager to become the "king-maker" who
made it so.

In 1889 Joseph B. Foraker was the Republican choice
for governor of Ohio; and although this was not a totally
satisfactory nomination within Republican circles, William
McKinley stuck to party lines and supported Foraker all the
way. In a way, one might say that Foraker dragged the party
down to defeat that year, for the other state candidates did
not fare well. And, of course, that next year McKinley lost
his seat in Congress through the gerrymandering of the
Democratic legislature. McKinley never whimpered, however, but settled down to work for the party. He was the
logical Republican candidate to run for governor in 1891,
and when the Republican state convention was held that
year, very little consideration was given to any other candidate.

The one person, apparently, who had little interest in
seeing McKinley run for governor was William McKinley.
Ohio in those years was run by the legislature. The governor had no veto power; he was an administrator, with only
advisory political powers. This did not appeal to McKinley
at all. He was not being coy; McKinley was never coy. He
always stated his position in politics, and when he wanted a
job he was very honest in saying so. He did not much want
the governorship.

There was another reason for his reluctance to run for governor. The incumbent, James E. Campbell, had defeated Foraker too handily and was too popular with the voters of Ohio for McKinley's taste. He could not stand another defeat for political office at this time. He had been defeated twice. Three times might well mean "out," and McKinley did not want to take the chance. Matters were further complicated by the tide of feeling, within even the Republican party of Ohio, against the high protective tariff. It was not so much that Ohio Republicans had ceased to believe in the tariff; but it was not working well, and many of them thought McKinley had taken matters too far, and that he ought to be put aside for that reason.

McKinley would have been perfectly happy to sit out politics for two or three years. Congress had interfered with his personal fortunes, and he was quite certain that if he returned to the practice of law he could make enough money in a few years to assure his family contentment and himself a trouble-free old age. Also, having received a handful of votes for the presidential nomination, he had the idea of the presidency very much in his mind. The timing for that had to be right; he had to be in proper position and strength. Defeat for governor of Ohio might end his hopes. The chance did not seem to be worth the risk.

Yet politics does not work quite that way. The man must consider his own needs; he must also consider the needs of his party, and in 1891 the Republicans of Ohio needed a man of proven ability and power to run for the governorship if they hoped to win that office back from the Democrats.

The state convention met in Columbus in June and William McKinley was nominated without difficulty. Then came a whirlwind campaign, in which the national issues of tariff and the currency were most important.

The election that followed was a close one. No one received a majority. Of the four candidates, the Prohibitionist ran last. The People's Party man ran third. Then came the Democrat and William McKinley, separated only by 21,000 votes, or about as many as the Prohibition and People's candidates both got. So it was a victory, but certainly not overwhelming, for William McKinley and the Republicans. The legislature was much more decisively Republican than anyone had hoped. Republicans outnumbered Democrats more than two to one in the senate, and almost two to one in the house of representatives.

One reason for the difficulties in which the Republican party found itself in this period was a serious breach within the party. A faction led by former-Governor Foraker had controlled the party in Ohio for some years. Mark Hanna wanted to break that control. In this election he succeeded, by electing enough members to the state senate to control the election of the next United States senator (who in those days was chosen by the state senate). In 1891 he saw to it that Senator John Sherman would be returned to Washington instead of Foraker, who wanted the post. Thus, while using his power, he earned the enmity of the Foraker faction.

This breach strengthened McKinley's position in the Ohio Republican party, because he stood apart from both factions and was regarded as the man who could unify the party. Again luck, combined with good judgment on McKinley's part, played an important role in his success.

McKinley is often regarded as the friend of big business because of his role in developing the high tariff; but that view is not entirely a fair one. As governor, when he observed the need for a new revenue system for Ohio to meet its growing needs, he proposed an excise tax on corporations which created new revenues and made it possible to

lower other taxes that struck individuals. Although he had
little direct power in legislation, he did have the right to
suggest legislation. He planned a law to improve safety on
railroads and tramways. He also asked for an arbitration
law (though, under it, arbitration was not compulsory) to
avoid strikes and labor disputes. Throughout his term he
comported himself with such dignity and success that when
the next election came in 1893 he received an absolute majority of votes, and a plurality of 80,000 votes over the
Democratic candidate.

His second administration was marked by serious labor
difficulties. Not only in Ohio, but all across the nation in
1894 and 1895, labor was beginning to organize seriously,
and employers wanted no dealings with labor unions. This
difficult situation led to many strikes and lockouts, and even
to violence. In the spring of 1894 there was a general strike
of miners in Ohio and other states, and the militia had to be
called out to try to avert property damage and threats to life
and limb. There were a number of lynchings, and in the
Hocking Valley as a result of the strike many miners and
their families came to the verge of starvation. When the
Governor learned how serious the condition of the people
in this region was, he ordered a railroad carload of provi-
sions sent to Nelsonville, prepared to pay for them himself.
When his friends assumed the cost, he contributed a considerable amount, and he also made a statewide appeal
through chambers of commerce and other organizations
that resulted in many supplies being brought to the area.
This was the only way he could help; in those days the
governor had no power to use state funds for relief of suffering of this type.

During McKinley's second term as governor he was very
much a candidate for the presidency, and his mentor in this
was Mark Hanna, the man who yearned to be a political

power behind the throne. McKinley went far afield from Ohio to attend and address political meetings. He travelled to Illinois, to Michigan, to New York, Nebraska, and Pennsylvania. He made after-dinner speeches anywhere and everywhere.

Again, McKinley was a lucky man. President Harrison had defeated James G. Blaine for the Republican presidential nomination in 1888, and by 1892 the pair was locked in deadly struggle for that same nomination. McKinley went to the convention in Minneapolis, along with Mark Hanna, to see if he could win the nomination as a dark horse in the race that was really between Harrison and Blaine. But Harrison walked away with the nomination, and McKinley was lucky that he did not get it; for the tide in America had turned against the Republican policies of taxation, and McKinley was the Democrats' Public Enemy Number One. Had he been a candidate that year, his career might well have ended right there.

As it was, McKinley was nearly ruined by his involvement in the financial affairs of a manufacturer whose unwise investments forced him into bankruptcy. This man was Robert L. Walker, an old school friend of McKinley's. McKinley was associated with him, although not as an active partner. Walker went broke, and McKinley was called upon to pay his debts. At first McKinley's political associates thought the debts amounted to around $25,000 and when McKinley said he must quit politics and go out to practice law, they subscribed that sum. Then it was learned that the total debts would be $130,000. McKinley paced the floor of his house and groaned about his fate. "I have kept clear of all entanglements all my life," he said. "Oh, that this should come to me now." He could see his dream of the presidency flying out the window.

Mrs. McKinley had an inheritance, which she turned

over to Mark Hanna because Hanna insisted on handling
McKinley's debts. In another era, McKinley would most
certainly have been ruined politically by this debt problem, or by the manner in which it was resolved; for Mark
Hanna and other powerful industrialists took over the
debt and paid almost all of it off. The Democrats attempted
to capitalize on McKinley's difficulties. They said McKinley should not be kept in public office because he could not
manage his own affairs properly. They did not, however,
raise the question of undue influence by the men who had
helped McKinley, because that was not the political style
of the times.

# CHAPTER 6

# The Election of 1896

EARLY IN THE WINTER of 1895 Mark Hanna rented a house in Thomasville, Georgia, and left the chill of Cleveland to spend the winter in the warmer climate. To those who wished to think so, this was the act of a wealthy man accommodating himself to his own pleasure. Actually, Hanna was preparing for the nomination of William McKinley at the Republican convention of 1896. Although by this year the South was solidly Democratic, still there was a Republican party there; and although the party was a helpless opposition, the Republican of the South had just as much power as his northern counterpart when it came to voting for a candidate for the nomination at the party's national convention. Hanna's plan was to line up the southern Republicans for McKinley, and then go into the convention with all the normal support of the Middle West and this southern support as well.

One of Hanna's first moves was to invite Governor McKinley and his wife to Thomasville to meet Republicans from all parts of the South. They stayed at Hanna's house for three weeks, and while they were there the southerners came to call. They liked the Ohio governor and his invalid wife (whose illness had now been discovered to be epilepsy).

McKinley was completely open about his presidential

ambitions among his friends, in private; but he was not ready to announce them to the world, no matter how often he was urged to by friendly Republican leaders. There was no mistaking his position, however, after the spring of 1895 when he accepted an invitation to speak in Hartford, Connecticut, from a group which had recently formed a McKinley-for-President club. Yet he still did not come out and say "I want to be President." Such a move would have been considered bad political form and would undoubtedly have hurt his chances of securing the nomination at the Republican convention of 1896; for the parties were to maintain a fiction for many years that the nomination sought the man and not otherwise. They pretended that the staunch and incorruptible convention delegates were ruled only by their heads, and not by any outside pressures or considerations, when it came to choosing the man they would like to see in the White House.

That autumn, when the election for governor came along, William McKinley campaigned heartily for Asa S. Bushnell, the candidate of the Foraker faction of Ohio Republicans. That faction had seized control of the state political convention and the party machinery while Mark Hanna was preoccupied with the grooming of McKinley for President. Yet the difficulty was Hanna's, not McKinley's, because the Governor was so popular in the state that all factions backed him for President when the matter was discussed at the state convention. This paved the way for McKinley to cement his relations with the Foraker men by backing Bushnell all the way. He travelled all over the state, speaking for Bushnell. Of course he was also showing himself to the people and speaking for McKinley too, but not in a way that anyone could disapprove. Bushnell, in the end, was elected by an even greater majority than McKinley had received in his second election, and much of the credit for this must be given the Governor and his speeches.

When 1896 rolled in, and the new governor Bushnell took office, McKinley made his farewell address to the state legislature, moved out of his rooms at the hotel across from the capitol, and returned to the house on North Market Street in Canton where he and Ida had lived for so long. He went into seclusion as far as the public was concerned; he did not make public speeches and he did not comment on public issues. But the political campaign for his nomination was more active than ever. A direct telephone line connected his library with Mark Hanna's office in Cleveland. His table, it was said, was set for a dozen guests at every meal. Republican leaders from near and far visited the house every day. Newspaper correspondents lurked on the porch, but without much luck. One woman reporter from the Philadelphia *Press* managed to interview Ida McKinley, who held court in the parlor, sitting in an overstuffed chair and speaking of her childhood and her romance with Major McKinley. But in the library, the Major was unapproachable by the press. It was in the tradition of politics then that the candidate not rock the boat by saying too much too soon about anything.

That is not to say that McKinley was not thinking about public affairs. He had shown himself to be a man much concerned with the wishes and welfare of the people. He came from a business community in the heart of a business-oriented state, and he thought of public welfare in terms of business welfare. But one of his favorite considerations when pondering any public matter was whether it was "right and fair and just." He was forever using these terms in his discussions with Mark Hanna about political matters.

All his life McKinley had a presence that seemed remarkable to others. One day he and Hanna went to a football game played between Yale and Princeton colleges. The crowd was as much interested in McKinley as he was in the game. Many said he looked like Napoleon (which he did, but a benign, friendly Napoleon).

McKinley was always loyal to his friends; indeed, the cause of his financial difficulties had been his loyalty. Robert Walker had raised the loans endorsed by McKinley nearly ten times in all, and McKinley made no public complaint although the affair drove him into actual bankruptcy.

McKinley was a man of great enthusiasms. Even in middle age, when most men are forgetting half their friends, McKinley made new attachments every year. He met Charles G. Dawes and George B. Cortelyou in his later political years, and they became his intimates. But McKinley was not a whole political figure, as Theodore Roosevelt or Grover Cleveland could be said to be. McKinley, as a national party leader, was the product of a new phenomenon in American politics: the creature of public relations. In her exhaustive study of the McKinley presidential years, Margaret Leech noted that only together did Mark Hanna and William McKinley make "one perfect politician." In front was McKinley, the party leader, the politician who could sense the public attitude even as it was forming, the speaker who could arouse his listeners, the moralist and the diplomat among warring factions. Standing behind him was Mark Hanna, the businessman, the organizer, the compromiser, and above all, the master publicist. "He has advertised McKinley," Theodore Roosevelt said, "as if he were a patent medicine."

By the fall of 1895 the McKinley-for-President campaign was steaming along. Hanna visited New York to confer jointly with two important political bosses, Matthew Quay of Pennsylvania and former-Senator Thomas Platt of New York.

These two leaders offered to support McKinley for the presidency at the convention, but their price was very high: Platt wanted to be Secretary of the Treasury and he wanted the promise in writing; Quay wanted control of at least one cabinet appointment. McKinley, when he learned from Hanna what the price was, said it was far too high. "If I cannot be President without promising to make Tom Platt Secretary of the Treasury," he said, "I will never be President."

So the support of Pennsylvania and New York was lost. Pennsylvania got behind Speaker of the House Tom Reed. New York's support would go to one of two other candidates. The important thing, however, was that these big city bosses had met and decided that no matter who received the nomination, it would not be McKinley; McKinley must be defeated, because he would not share the spoils of success with these bosses, or on the terms they wished it shared.

In a way, William McKinley was lucky not to have the support of the bosses of the big city political machines. There was a new air in American politics: it had begun blowing when Garfield came into office and talked about cleaning up the civil service system; it had become a good breeze in the days of Cleveland, the incorruptible. The public—the people who voted—had a strong distaste for the plug-hatted, cigar-chewing, deal-making politician who walked about the city streets handing out dollar bills and jobs in the sewers. McKinley had taken a high moral tone in dealing with the politicians, and now Hanna, the political organizer, made good use of his candidate's position. He let political groups everywhere know that McKinley had turned down the support of the bosses because they had asked for cabinet posts, while McKinley was determined to choose "the best men" for the jobs. McKinley-for-President clubs sprouted up in New York and Pennsylvania. They grew very powerful in the Middle West. Hanna was very busy all spring advertising the McKinley campaign as the campaign of the people against the party bosses.

With the growth of his power in the Republican party, McKinley became the subject of much attention in the press and a strange myth began to develop about him. It was easy to see how it came about, given the relationship between McKinley and Hanna, without an understanding of McKinley's character. The Hearst newspapers in particular started after McKinley. They could find no scandal about him. His personal life was an open book. He had been a war hero. His public career was honest, and he had taken strong stands on various difficult issues, such as the purchase of silver (which brought support in the mountain states). The one issue on which he could be faulted was his handling of finances. The antagonistic press picked this up and charged that he was the creature of Hanna and the other industrialists because he did not know how to spend a dollar, or to save one.

Another weapon was used against McKinley. This was the spear of suspicion, and it was brought against him by the libeling of Mark Hanna. Hanna was depicted everywhere among McKinley's enemies as a bloated plutocrat who was itching to get his hands on control of the White House. He was shown in cartoons as a dirty, dishonest figure covered with moneybags and dollar signs; as a puppet master with McKinley as his puppet; as an organ grinder with McKinley as his monkey.

All this propaganda was most unfair to McKinley and to Hanna. True, Hanna went to see the politicians and heard their requests. He brought these to McKinley, and McKinley made the decisions as to what he would do and what he would not do. He did not abandon his moral principles or his high ideals.

As the spring wore on, many pressures were brought to

bear on William McKinley and Mark Hanna. There was an organization called the American Protective Association which was for "100 percent Americanism" and against Catholics, Jews, and all foreigners. McKinley had locked horns with this group during his two terms as governor because he had refused to discriminate against anyone on such grounds in making appointments to public office. Now the A.P.A. did its best to hurt him. Rumors were spread and anonymous papers were written about his secret adherence to the Roman Catholic religion. (This was untrue. McKinley was not anti-Catholic, but he had no affiliation with that belief.) The anonymous letter-writers said McKinley was opposed to public education, preferring parochial schools, that his appointments as governor had been dictated by the Catholic Bishop of Columbus, that he had sent his own two children to be educated in a convent. Some formal denials of these untruthful charges were made by the McKinley office in Canton, but for the most part William McKinley suffered them in silence, noting to friends and relatives that it was sad that in the American political system a man was attacked for his religious beliefs, and even sadder when the officials of a secret society sat in judgment on a public official and were able to influence voters.

It was not McKinley's way to strike back openly against the A.P.A. He did not choose to engage in any arguments at this point in his political career. He proposed to seek the Republican nomination on the basis of his public record, believing that his chances of hurting himself were worse if he said anything at all than if he did not defend himself against charges or commit himself to new causes.

McKinley's candidacy was hurt, in this respect, because he would not speak out on the important issue of money and currency. The Democrats were engaged in a loud public argument about the problem of "Free Silver," which was to be such an important aspect of the campaign of 1896. Eighteen years earlier the Bland-Allison Act had required the Treasury to buy at least two million dollars', but not more than four million dollars', worth of silver every month. All this silver was to be purchased at the current market price and was then to be coined into silver money. Originally the law had been proposed by the advocates of unlimited coinage of silver, but by 1890 the four-million-dollar limitation placed on the law during debate in Congress had frustrated the aims of the group that was known as the Silver Bloc. In the twelve years between 1878 and 1890, so much silver was discovered in the mines of the world, and so much of it was brought out to be used as currency in Austria, India, China, Mexico, and other countries besides the United States, that the price of silver kept falling in relation to the much scarcer gold. By 1890 an ounce of silver was worth one-twentieth the value of an ounce of gold—or to put it in a way the metal men liked to talk, the ratio was 20 to 1.

At that time, four new states in the West had been admitted to the Union; and each of these four had hope, if not actual proof, of the presence of considerable amounts of silver ore in the territory. So, in both House and Senate, the forces that advocated heavier use of silver money were growing stronger. That year, when the McKinley Tariff Act came up, in a compromise measure (which McKinley had supported) the Sherman Silver Purchase Act was passed. This new law provided for the purchase of four and a half million ounces of silver every month and the issuance of paper money against it. What really happened was that the paper issued against the silver was redeemable in silver *or* gold. Soon the bankers and foreign traders were buying silver, selling it to the government for paper money, redeeming that paper money in gold, and buying more silver

McKinley (second from right) in front of his house in Canton, Ohio, 1896

McKinley delivering his first inaugural address, 1897

Mrs. William McKinley in her sitting room in the White House

McKinley campaign button

Cartoon of McKinley's administration, ham-strung by pressure groups (1897)

Drawing of the explosion of the battleship "Maine" in Havana harbor, February 15, 1898

The United States fleet, led by Admiral Dewey, defeats the Spanish fleet at the Battle of Manila, August 13, 1898

Cartoon of President McKinley and his protege Mark Hanna (1899): Pointing to the portrait of Henry Clay, who said "I would rather be right than President," Hanna is saying to McKinley, "That man Clay was an ass. It's better to be President than to be right!"

Assassination of President McKinley at the Pan-American Exposition in Buffalo, New York, September 6, 1901

with the gold, which kept a steady drain on the national gold supply while the amount of silver kept piling up in the federal vaults. President Cleveland had opposed such a measure and now, in the Harrison administration, he was proved correct. The huge government surplus of money, in four short years, was converted to a huge deficit. In 1893, during the second Cleveland administration, the Sherman Silver Purchase Act was repealed.

This repeal caused a serious split in the ranks of the Democratic party. The leaders of the Silver Bloc were Senator Edward Teller, and Representatives Richard P. Bland and William Jennings Bryan. During 1895 a number of independent conventions of silver men were held around the country, sometimes causing political leaders to cross party lines.

In the spring of 1896 the silver men pleaded with McKinley to come out in favor of their position. He said that his position was perfectly clear from the public statements he had made in the past and he had nothing more to say on the subject of currency. But what *was* his position? Reading his various statements over the years, one could decide that he was for unlimited silver coinage or that he was for strict adherence to a "sound money" or strong gold policy. At various times he had indicated support for both positions.

This refusal to come out either in favor of silver or in favor of a strong gold policy caused much unrest within the Republican party, and was the most dangerous fault of the early McKinley campaign for the presidency.

The Republican National Convention was to meet in St. Louis on June 16. Late in May the Prohibition party had met in Pittsburgh and nominated its slate of candidates. The Prohibition party was a protest party, a nuisance to the regular politicians and very little more than that. But

in 1896 there was something to be learned from the actions
of the Prohibitionists' convention. Usually the Prohibitionists were held together by their bonds of belief in the evil of
strong drink for all mankind. In 1896 the Prohibition party
split in two, not on the issue of drink, but on the issue of
free silver, and one segment of the party deserted the fold
to nominate its own candidates, under the name of the
National party. The National party, like the Prohibitionists, believed in outlawing liquor; but it also believed in
unlimited coinage of silver as a solution to the nation's
economic problems.

Mark Hanna and William McKinley finally were forced
to take cognizance of the silver question. McKinley submitted a statement which came out for sound money, with
silver used to the fullest extent consistent with the maintenance of its parity with gold. This really did not mean
anything except that the Republican party, if it followed
McKinley's wishes, would not support absolutely unlimited
coinage of silver.

McKinley did not wish to come out more strongly because he had the tentative support of the western silver
bloc, and he wanted to keep it. Mark Hanna went to St.
Louis a few days before the convention opened, and there
he quickly learned that the eastern bankers and businessmen were very much worried about McKinley's failure to
take a stronger stand for the maintenance of the gold standard and "sound money."

The Republican convention considered the names of
candidates on June 18, and there was really none other than
William McKinley, so well had Mark Hanna done his
work. When the first ballot was announced and Alabama
cast its 18 votes for McKinley, the rush began, and it did not
take long. Before the candidates' names were announced,
the party had approved the platform, and the platform not

only did not come out for unlimited coinage of silver; it mentioned for the first time that the gold standard should be retained, which was a much stronger way than usual of saying that unlimited coinage was out of the question.

McKinley was at home in Canton, wandering about his house, listening occasionally to a second-hand report of the convention proceedings over a telephone connection especially installed for that purpose. Canton was decorated with flags and bunting, and thousands of people had come into town from all the little villages and farms around because there was no question in their minds that McKinley would be nominated. Bands came to play, and organized crowds besieged the house, including a crowd from Masillon which arrived by special train. McKinley made speeches from the front porch, from the back porch, and inside the house. Between five o'clock that afternoon and midnight, it was estimated that he addressed 50,000 people and shook hands with a great number of them.

McKinley's closest competitor in this contest was Thomas Reed, Speaker of the House of Representatives, the candidate of a hard-money group of easterners. But actually McKinley now also represented the gold standard, and he carried the nomination on the first ballot.

As it turned out, the election of 1896 was one of those infrequent ones in which a matter of public policy was more important than the personality of the candidate. It was made so by the action of the Democratic party when it met at Chicago on July 7; the silver bloc of Democrats, stampeded by a powerful orator named William Jennings Bryan, quickly nominated him for President on a platform of support of coinage of silver and restraint of the big business interests of the East. There was some hope among the Democrats that they could thus secure the support of the Republicans of the West who favored free coinage of silver.

That hope was realized on July 22 when Senator Henry Teller of Colorado and a number of other Republicans from the West met in St. Louis and endorsed the Democratic platform and the Democratic candidate for 1896.

It was apparent to Republicans as well as to Democrats that if the election for President had been held in the summer of 1896, William Jennings Bryan would have won by a landslide. Mark Hanna would not have it so, and he set to work to build an organization from the wormy, rotten wood of the Republican city machines and the odd lots of planking from the rural areas. The Republican bosses of the East, who had opposed McKinley because they could not have their way with him, suddenly became frightened of what might happen to their regions and their power if Bryan came into office. They truly pictured him in their own minds as a madman bent on bringing anarchy and bankruptcy to the United States.

The Republicans raised a large campaign fund, most of which was expended in the Middle West because this, Hanna recognized, was the great uncommitted area in which McKinley would either lose or win the election, depending on Hanna's power to organize the campaign. The East, with much grumbling, had moved behind McKinley, assisted by Grover Cleveland's dislike of Bryan and the Democratic platform of the period. Many conservative Democrats in the East were supporting the Republicans. The Far West was lost on the issue of silver. The Middle West, where Bryan was making hay in the hot summer, was the place to fight.

A Republican campaign fund of three and a half million dollars was raised in a few weeks, the largest amount of money ever gathered by a political party in America for a single campaign. It was raised in the East to be spent in the West.

The problem, as far as the Republicans were concerned, was to give a quick and convincing course in simple economics. The Republican position was, or could be made, convincing if the dangers of inflation and "free silver" could be explained to the people. Hanna undertook to do this in a few weeks. William Allen White, editor of the Emporia *Gazette*, wrote a pamphlet called "What's The Matter With Kansas?" which exposed these dangers. Mark Hanna arranged for the printing and distribution of a million copies of this pamphlet. The dangers of inflation to pensioners, people with insurance policies, and people with savings accounts was shown in schoolhouse meetings, stump sessions, and in articles in country newspapers. Hanna sent hundreds of paid speakers into the Middle West, and armed them with many tons of campaign material printed in a half-dozen languages.

William Jennings Bryan travelled all across the country like a whirlwind, speaking forcefully and attracting the voters. Had the campaign been left to that and William McKinley's "front porch" campaign, the Republicans would have been drowned in the tide, because McKinley saw it as his role to play the dignified statesman to Bryan's angry young man, and determined that he would not make a public appeal for votes, but would hold himself available on his front porch for informal meetings with Republicans who wished to see him. This retiring approach was possible only because Mark Hanna was doing just the opposite, and very effectively. Hanna went everywhere, with his army and his ammunition, while McKinley sat on the porch every day except Sunday and spoke to visitors from there.

This campaign was not a dud, as one might expect. The Republican National Committee arranged for such low excursion train fares to Canton that the Cleveland *Plain Dealer* said it was cheaper to go see McKinley than it was to stay at home. Once the crowd of farmers or lodgemen or workers arrived, McKinley greeted them courteously and shook hands. Then he got up on a chair and made a campaign speech, carefully tailored to the special interests of the particular group. The visitors then went home, and each of them told his friends and neighbors how he had shaken the great man's hand and how the candidate had addressed himself specifically to the political issues that were important to their region or their special interests. It was, when multiplied a thousand times, a very effective kind of campaign assuming that enough people came to the McKinley front porch to spread the word at home.

As the campaign progressed, McKinley admitted—without ever apologizing—that he had mistaken the major issue of 1896. It was not the McKinley Tariff. It was and must be the silver issue. He came around slowly but surely to a strong position against the unlimited use of silver; and so the fears of the gold standard men were allayed, strengthening the Republican position considerably.

After McKinley made his acceptance speech, the crowds of people who came to Canton increased, until on the last Saturday in September special trains brought more than 20,000 persons to hear McKinley address them in small groups. He spoke to eleven different gatherings that day, and a week later he talked sixteen times to a total of 30,000 people. McKinley's front porch campaign was so successful that the front porch threatened to fall down, the posts had been so weakened by the pressures of the crowds. The McKinley grape arbor had been picked clean of fruit, and the front lawn had been trodden into a sea of dust which became mud in the rains. Inside the house, an old friend would scarcely have recognized the furnishings because so many of the visitors had brought gifts for the candidate which he could not, in good faith, refuse.

He had to find places for such valuables as the largest
sheet of tin ever rolled in America, the largest sheet of iron,
canes, watermelons, moose heads, gavels, ceremonial pots,
flowers, and five live eagles named Major, McKinley, President, Hobart (after the vice-presidential candidate Garret
A. Hobart of New Jersey), and Hanna.

As election day grew closer the frenzy of the campaign
mounted. The Republicans sent industrialists to the Middle West. Mark Hanna made several speeches himself from
the back car of trains. Chauncey Depew, president of the
New York Central Railroad, took to his trains for speaking
engagements. Senator Foraker came home from Europe and
made a speaking tour.

By the first of November it was apparent that the Democrats controlled the South and the Far West, as everyone
had expected they would. But what had happened in the
great Middle West? Men had been persuaded, in one way
or another, that free silver would bring disaster. Some of
these people had been persuaded by Mark Hanna's propaganda, directly. Other groups had been persuaded indi-
rectly, as the workers in one factory who were warned by
their employer that if Bryan was elected they shouldn't
bother to show up for work the next day, because the factory
would be closed down. There was much more of this than
might be suspected, and it represents an ignoble side of the
Republican campaign and of the history of American politics. But it also was a measure of the fears that William
Jennings Bryan aroused with the ever more radical speeches
he was making in his desperate bid for election. He lam-
basted the "interests" (meaning big business) every day, and
indicated that big business must be brought under control
even if it meant government ownership of big industry.
This frightened many men, who began to believe that
Bryan really was, as Wall Streeters said, an "anarchist" and

that if he was elected the nation would fall apart, robbers and rapists would roam the streets at will, and no man's slender savings or property would be safe. In those days most Americans did not differentiate between anarchism and socialism.

The election was held on November 5. Just before election day the price of wheat went sky-high, and so did the price of other commodities. This was a crowning blow in the industrial areas, where the Republicans shouted in glee that already the inflationists of the West were beginning to take advantage of their hopes. The tide of free silver had turned in three months, due largely to the huge amount of money spent by Mark Hanna in educating and persuading the people, by fair means and foul. By midnight on election day the results were in, or at least enough of them to let it be known in Canton, Ohio, that William McKinley had been elected President of the United States.

# CHAPTER 7

# The First Term

"OH GOD, keep him humble," said William Mc-
Kinley's mother when she heard the welcome news that her
son had just been elected President of the United States.
She need not have worried, for many men had come to the
office of President wearing arrogance on their sleeves, only
to be humbled by the office; because no man could stand
alone and still occupy that office with dignity and wisdom,
nor could any man alone reach all the right conclusions
about the problems that faced him or make all the right
decisions. And there were always the press, Congress, and
the public who would be quick to point out the places
where he had erred.

The first task of the new President was to choose the
administrators with which he would surround himself—his
secretaries of the various federal departments who would
comprise his cabinet. In McKinley's case this selection
took four months, during which he studied many situations
and was subjected to many pressures.

In 1896, while proclaiming themselves advocates of the
traditional American policy of isolation from world affairs,
the Republicans and American businessmen were really not
isolationists at all but were moving rapidly to seek new markets for American goods abroad. In the nineteenth century

this meant America must pursue a policy of international intervention in the affairs of weaker peoples, which was termed imperialism at one stage and colonialism at another.

There was no other effective way to secure new markets abroad; for imperialism was the policy of the great colonial powers, England, France, Germany, Spain, Portugal, and the new power, Japan. The colonial powers moved into island kingdoms and defenseless republics and made them vassals of the mother countries. In every case the political affairs of the lesser land were tied closely to the economic interests of the mother country. Only in China had this process of chopping up helpless nations into colonies been circumvented, largely because of the stubbornness of the Chinese, the intervention of the Americans years before in behalf of the Open Door policy—or free trade for America —and the jealousies among the foreigners in China. Britain had seized Hong Kong and held it. The Russians had seized parts of Manchuria. The Germans had seized the tip of the Shantung peninsula, but in Shanghai, up the Yangtze River, and along the eastern coastline the foreigners controlled in common, not singly. Africa was split among the British, French, and Germans, with some Italian and Spanish and Portuguese holdings of lesser importance. Latin America was freeing itself from the Spanish yoke, and so were certain areas in the Caribbean. For the most part the available weaker kingdoms were taken up, so if the United States wished to pursue an eager search of foreign markets, she must take colonies from some of the weaker imperialist nations. There were a few islands and island groups left, particularly in Polynesia, where the multiplicity of foreign interests, including American, had kept any one nation from seizing control. Principal among the weaker colonial nations was Spain, and principal among the uncommitted markets was the kingdom, now republic, of Hawaii.

American business was in an aggressive mood in the 1890's because the last frontier—the West coast—had been tapped, and the backwash of immigration had lapped eastward again to fill the gaps in the Rocky Mountain region. There was much talk about America having gone about as far as it could go, much worry about exploitation of resources. The Guggenheims were moving into Mexico, and were exploring the cold country of Canada and Alaska to find and exploit mineral resources. Traders were actively searching for new markets south and east and west.

In the second Cleveland administration, pressure had been brought by Congress to expand America into an imperial position. Cleveland had resisted, but when he also resisted the British attempt to take over the Republic of Venezuela, his strong talk about possible American military action gave comfort to the expansionist Congress. Congress was attempting to force Spain to abandon her colony of Cuba, and Congress had passed a resolution demanding the recognition of the revolutionaries in Cuba. In the political platforms of both parties in 1896 the Cuban question had been raised, and both parties had expressed a sympathy with the revolutionaries against Spain. It would not be proper to ascribe all this to a purely selfish business interest; there were Americans of revolutionary spirit who recalled the beginnings of America and wanted to encourage the true independence of Cuba. But their motivation was not the primary one among the people who framed the political platforms of the parties. The possibilities of trade and the interests of American businessmen were very much in that picture.

There was also the matter of an isthmian canal. The French had failed in their effort to build a canal across the Panamanian part of the isthmus, but it was quite apparent that the pressures of all nations for such a facility were growing rapidly and that the larger powers would all like to control the isthmian canal. If the United States did not protect its interests here (and nobody seriously considered the interests of Panama or Nicaragua, the two isthmian nations), then the bigger and more powerful nations would step in and the United States' Monroe Doctrine would not be worth a nickel.

For all these reasons the selection of the Secretary of State was the primary consideration of the new President. There was another reason: the Secretary of State was the most important cabinet official, for if the President died and the Vice-President died, then the Secretary of State became the next in line for the presidency.

McKinley's first choice for Secretary of State was Senator William Allison of Iowa—not because he knew anything about foreign affairs (which he did not), but because he was an important middle-western Republican leader, representing a very important bloc of votes, and one of the most senior and most powerful men in the United States Senate. He was chairman of the Senate Finance Committee, which exercised almost as much influence on the acceptance of the federal budget submitted by the administration as did the House Committee on Ways and Means. It probably would have been an excellent appointment, because Allison was a diplomat by nature; but he had no taste for an appointive job in the cabinet when he exercised his power so successfully in the Senate, and he refused to be considered.

McKinley, then, was reduced to looking around for second choices, and this meant listening to the arguments of his advisors. Principal among these was Mark Hanna, who wanted to become a United States senator. Like Allison, he recognized the superior and more impregnable position of an official responsible to someone other than the President. He had made McKinley President, but he was wise enough to know how little real influence he had on the new President's affairs and how easily kingmakers could be tossed aside if they did not protect their flanks. So Hanna's ambitions turned toward a seat in the United States Senate, and he knew how to obtain one rather easily. Let the President appoint the respected elder statesman, John Sherman, to the office of Secretary of State. That appointment would create a vacancy in the United States Senate delegation from Ohio, and since McKinley had so eagerly supported the new governor of Ohio and Hanna was boss of the Ohio party, it was not too much to ask that Mark Hanna be appointed junior senator to fill that vacancy.

Senator Sherman was seventy-four years old that year, and on the face of it he would make an admirable Secretary of State. He had served for a decade on the Foreign Relations Committee. He had been a candidate for the presidential nomination a number of times and, although never winning, he had conducted himself always with a dignity that lent him a huge public following as a statesman. His one major problem was a certain heaviness of hand, a tendency to shoot from the hip in pronouncements on delicate issues.

Sherman was offered the post and was very pleased to accept it. Senator Foraker, leader of the Ohio Republican faction that hated Hanna, tried to prevent Hanna's appointment to the Senate post, but McKinley intervened in favor of his campaign manager, and the matter was settled.

The first post in the cabinet, then, went for political reasons to a man not particularly suited for it temperamentally, and to satisfy the ambitions of one of McKinley's backers.

Next came the appointment of the Secretary of War, considered to be the second most powerful place in the cabinet. McKinley chose Russell A. Alger of Michigan, an important Republican leader and a very wealthy man who had nearly nothing else to recommend him. The fiscal problems of the nation made the selection of the Secretary of the Treasury very important. An unwise secretary might wreck the credit of the United States or allow the advocates of "good money" to go too far in protecting the currency. McKinley considered several men and finally chose Lyman J. Gage for the post. Gage was a Chicago banker and a Democrat, but he was very definitely a sound money man and a good administrator. John D. Long, a Harvard man and a lawyer, became Secretary of the Navy. Joseph Mc-Kenna of California, a Roman Catholic, was given the post of Attorney-General—not because McKinley was showing particular favor or courage, but because he liked McKenna and quite forgot about his religion until he had decided to make the appointment. Then McKinley showed courage, because he shrugged off complaints of the extremists.

When the cabinet was complete the selections were announced to the press, and on March 1, 1897, William Mc-Kinley and a party of about fifty persons left Canton for Washington. The party rode in a special seven-car train on the Pennsylvania Railroad. When they arrived in Washington the McKinleys went to the Ebbitt House on F Street to prepare for the inaugural ceremonies after which the McKinleys would move into the White House. Then McKinley went to the White House to dine and to have a private talk with the man he was replacing as chief executive. This custom had originated a few years before, and McKinley was glad to follow it for he truly admired Grover Cleveland.

On the day that the McKinleys came to the White House, Cleveland was suffering from an attack of gout; but he stumped down the stairs with a bandage on his foot, and he and McKinley talked about pressing national issues. Cleveland was convinced now that war had become almost cer-

tain because of the overwhelming war feeling in Congress.
The war party at this time consisted of both Democrats and
Republicans, without regard to anything save feelings for
expansion of American power and super-patriotism. A very
serious situation had developed in Havana, where the
American consul was engaged in conspiracies against the
Spanish authorities. Cleveland described this problem to
McKinley in sombre terms and warned him about the con-
duct of General Fitzhugh Lee, who was the consul there.
He suggested that unless Spain could be persuaded to sell
Cuba to the United States there would be conflict very soon,
and he urged McKinley to put his closest attention to the
problem of keeping the peace. But he had no confidence
that it could be done, in any case.

McKinley could not bring himself to take so gloomy a
view of the situation. He and Cleveland shared the hope
that international arbitration could be established as a
means of settling all disputes among nations. McKinley
remarked that he had put a sentence in his inaugural address praising the agreement that had been reached with
Britain, which Cleveland had just sent to the Senate for
approval. He added that he would do everything he could
to keep relations with Spain on a friendly basis.

Two days later, on March 4, 1897, McKinley entered a
carriage, drove to the White House and picked up Cleveland, and moved on to the Capitol for his inauguration.
"We want no wars of conquest," he said in his inaugural
speech. "We must avoid the temptation of territorial ag-
gression." He also spoke of other problems he intended to
deal with in the near future: civil service reform, restora-
tion of the Merchant Marine, control of trusts.

Then came the inaugural parade, led by General Horace
Porter, who had been U. S. Grant's military aide, and then
the inaugural ball.

The next day it was down to business for the new Presi-

dent of the United States. One of the first problems he had
to face was a growling from Republicans about jobs. In the
Cleveland administration 80,000 federal jobs had been put
under civil service, which meant that half the total number
were not available to the party as rewards for political loyalty. Thirty thousand of these positions had *just* been put
under civil service, hastily, by Cleveland to bolster his constant program of civil service reform. In this action some
mistakes had been made so that, for example, the cabinet
members could not even choose their own private secretaries. McKinley knew that he was going to face a very unfriendly Congress on this subject, but he did not wish to
give any ground to the old spoilsmen. So he laid aside the
question of exceptions to the new rule until a later date
and addressed other problems.

One of these was a matter with which he was as well
fitted to deal as any man in the nation. It was the establishment of a working relationship with Congress. In the
House the Republicans were in control, so the leadership
of Speaker Thomas Reed was not impaired. The House
could be managed. The Senate presented a different problem. The Republicans in the Senate in the Fifty-fifth Congress seemed to hold a handsome majority: there were fifty-
five Republican Senators, thirty-four Democrats, five Populists, and two silver men. But that apparent strength did
not represent the true condition, because many of those
Republicans were Republicans in name but silver men in
fact. And the Senate was split across party lines in the other
matter of expansionism.

From the beginning, foreign affairs created the most
pressing problems for the new President in his cabinet
meetings. Foremost was the problem of Spain and Cuba;
but that was not the only matter of American interests
abroad which faced the new government. The United States

and Canada were in disagreement over the use of the Ber-
ing Sea fisheries because the increasing hunting of seals for
their fur was threatening the seal herds. At this time there
was no direct route of negotiation between Washington
and Ottawa. Instead, American-Canadian relations were
handled in London, between Ambassador Hay and the colonial secretary at the British foreign office. It was a most
unsatisfactory system. The British did not want to talk
about the matter or to submit it to arbitration; and meanwhile, year after year, the Canadian seal hunters were cut-
ting down the herds.

Other serious problems of foreign affairs faced this new
administration, one of which was the fate of American
interests in Pago Pago, in the Samoan Islands group.
Twenty years earlier the United States had begun to acquire
commercial and territorial interests in Samoa. The Germans had begun their drive for colonies at that time, and
there had been a time, in 1889, when war seemed very close
between the United States and Germany. Indeed, a typhoon
which had wrecked an American and a German flotilla may
have been responsible for the preservation of the peace
then. After that, German, American, and British interests
had agreed to establish a three-way protectorate over Samoa.
It was not working very well by 1897.

Another problem concerned the Hawaiian Islands. The
United States had established a naval base at Pearl Harbor
in the Hawaiian Islands and had considerable economic interests in the islands. Spurred on by commercial interests,
a group of missionary families and planters had staged a
revolution against the Hawaiian kingdom in 1893, expecting then that Hawaii would be annexed to the United States.
The American consul in Hawaii had been party to the plot,
and when President Cleveland had learned of this he had
become outraged and had quite refused to have anything

to do with annexation (although at the very end of the
Harrison administration a treaty had been drawn, and the
bloc that favored annexation had hoped they were present-
ing the next President, Cleveland, with a *fait accompli*).
President McKinley was of another view. He believed that
Hawaii would be valuable to the United States; and since
he had not been a party to the original scheming which
caused the overthrow of Hawaii's Queen Liliuokalani, he
favored the negotiation of a new treaty of annexation. The
time was not ripe for it because the Senate was much more
concerned about the Cuban problem at the moment, but
McKinley put the wheels in motion for Hawaiian annexation anyhow.

That year the Japanese were beginning to move in
Hawaii. They had watched the maneuvers of the Americans
and had seen that Cleveland had rejected the motion to take
Hawaii into the United States' sphere of political as well
as economic influence. The Japanese population of Hawaii
was growing rapidly, and Japan's own was growing so much
that the need for constant expansion was felt in the home
islands. In the month that McKinley took office the Japanese sent a thousand emigrants to Hawaii; and so concerned were the Hawaiian authorities that they turned the
ships around and sent them straight back to Japan. Japan's
government became enraged and sent a cruiser to Hawaiian
waters with a demand for indemnification of those who had
lost money in the attempt to settle in the islands.

In June, 1897, matters came to a serious pass. In that
month the American minister in Honolulu completed the
drafting and signing of a treaty of annexation with the
Hawaiian Republic, which was headed by people of American birth. Threatening noises came immediately from the
Japanese foreign office. Three American warships were
sent to Hawaii to join the Japanese warship that lay in the
harbor. The message was plain.

So concerned about the future of the Hawaiian Islands did Minister Harold Sewall become that he asked for permission to land a force on the islands just in case the Japanese did so, and to declare a provisional American protectorate over the islands while the Senate was considering the treaty of annexation. The State Department and President McKinley were not very eager to authorize so strong an action, even in case of outright Japanese interference, but in the end they did so. Minister Sewall said later that the reason there was no incident was because the United States had taken so strong a stand. He was certain that the Japanese had knowledge of his secret instructions just as soon as he did, because American security was so poor in those days. He felt that the Japanese knew the landing of United States troops would mean at least a local war with the United States, and this kept them from landing their troops.

Although the administration was concerned about the problems of Hawaii, little time could be spent on them. Most attention was given to trying to settle the differences with Spain. Every day the newspapers carried reports of new troubles and new atrocities in Cuba. The people of America were becoming very seriously aroused and so was Congress.

McKinley had one difficulty from the beginning: given the state of public opinion, no responsible person wanted to take on the job of minister to Spain. It was several months before McKinley could persuade a fitting candidate, General Stewart L. Woodford, to undertake the job. Woodford sailed for the Iberian peninsula with instructions to tell the Spanish government that the fighting in Cuba must end immediately, because millions of dollars' worth of American property was being destroyed and American public opinion was inflamed. Even as he was on the high seas, something happened which facilitated his mission. The premier of Spain, Canogas del Castillo, was assassinated. His successor, Premier Sagasta, proved to be much more reasonable about the question of Cuba than Castillo. He ordered the release of all prisoners in Cuba who were American citizens, recalled the cruel governor, General Weyler, and replaced him with another general who was ordered to try to bring peace.

In December, 1897, President McKinley delivered his annual message to Congress, devoting most of it to the problems of Cuba and American relations with Spain. He discussed the cruelties of the Castillo regime in some detail, but he also said that the Sagasta government promised to do much to reform the situation in Cuba. He asked Congress to suspend judgment on the matter and do nothing that might slow the reforms promised or create difficulties between the United States and Spain. Instead of military intervention, he said, it was time for more humane measures. He had secured permission from the Spanish government for America to send supplies and medicines to relieve the suffering people of Cuba; and just before Christmas the State Department invited the public to contribute to a Cuban relief fund, which the President led off with a subscription of $5000 of his own. Considering his personal finances, this was a very large sum for him to contribute, and it indicated how strongly he felt about the problems of the suffering in Cuba and the relationship of Cuba to the United States.

CHAPTER 8

# The Spanish-American War

No sooner had President William McKinley appointed Senator John Sherman to be Secretary of State than he realized it was a mistake—now that it was too late to do anything about it without creating many wrong impressions. McKinley liked Sherman, and there was nothing dishonest or improper about the man; but the truth was that the old man was now senile and could not remember what was happening in the world around him from one day to the next. Sometimes in cabinet meetings he roused long enough to show flashes of the bright mind that had led him so far in the United States Senate. But flashes of brilliance will not run a federal department entrusted with the delicate matters of negotiating on a day to day basis with all other countries in the world. As a Secretary of State, John Sherman turned out to be a disaster.

He began by telling the Japanese minister to Washington that the United States had no intention of annexing Hawaii, even as a treaty of annexation was being drawn up. When it was made public, the Japanese lost faith in the honesty of the Secretary.

He gave an interview to the anti-McKinley New York *World,* stating that Japan was dangerous, England was full of bluff, and Spain was going to lose Cuba. This talk sur-

prised the Japanese; irritated the English; and infuriated
the Spanish, who were simply waiting for American interference in Cuba, quite sure that it was intended and would
come no matter how many assurances they had from
McKinley's minister in Madrid.

After that interview, Secretary Sherman had very little
prestige at home or abroad, and this was to become an important matter in the conduct of foreign policy in the next
few months.

Foreign policy is also a matter that touches closely on
military and naval policy. The Secretary of the Navy, John
D. Long, was a sensible and peaceable man. In those days
the position of admiral had been abolished to save money,
and the civilian secretary and his civilian assistant ran the
department without much help from career officers, who
were involved in the mechanical and professional side of
naval affairs. Theodore Roosevelt, Assistant Secretary of the
Navy, was an ardent interventionist who believed strongly
that the United States was destined to become an important
colonial power. To accomplish this, he wanted a strong,
two-ocean navy (which the United States most certainly did
not have), and he began to agitate for one. Secretary Long
did not like Roosevelt's talk, and told him so. Roosevelt
promised to behave, but it was impossible for him to con-
ceal his true feelings; and whenever the Secretary was out
of town and Roosevelt was in charge, he took actions which
furthered the cause of a strong navy. He wanted a squadron
to be sent to the Pacific, and he wanted Commodore George
Dewey to be given the command—mostly because Dewey
agreed with Roosevelt's view that war with Spain was in-
evitable, and that it must be fought to a successful conclusion on the sea.

At a dinner at the White House, Roosevelt talked plainly
about the coming war with Spain, and indicated that when

it came the Asiatic squadron should blockade Manila, in the Spanish possession of the Philippines, immediately. McKinley, knowing there must be a plan, just in case of war, agreed that this should be Commodore Dewey's program. McKinley, however, was not convinced that there was going to be a war with Spain. Everything he and his minister in Madrid were doing was calculated to settle the problems without war.

One of McKinley's problems was Secretary Sherman. Another was General Fitzhugh Lee, the consul in Havana, against whom former-President Cleveland had warned him. Either McKinley was too busy to pay any attention to the warning, or he believed in Lee. So he kept him in office, and Lee continued to scheme with the Cuban revolutionaries against the Spanish—which might not have been so bad had not the Spanish authorities in Madrid been thoroughly aware of the activities and concluded that McKinley was obviously playing two different games.

In the second week of January, 1898, General Lee sent reports of the unrest in Cuba back to Washington, and the growth of this unrest was sufficient to order the North Atlantic Squadron of the navy and a flotilla of torpedo boats to begin drilling practice off the coast of Florida. The "Maine," a heavy armed cruiser, was ordered to Key West. She was painted white, and she bore two smokestacks proudly above her multiple decks and big guns.

At this point McKinley decided to send American warships into Cuban waters—partly as a resumption of relations with the Cuban (Spanish) government which had been suspended by the Cleveland administration in protest against Spanish cruelties in Cuba, and partly as a gentle reminder that American might was on hand to protect American interests in Cuba should the need arise. This was done with the full knowledge and assent of Minister

Dupuy de Lome, the Spanish representative in Washington. So the "Maine" was sent to Havana, and the cruiser "Montgomery" was dispatched to pay courtesy calls at Santiago and Matanzas.

When the American consul at Havana reported this news to the Spanish government there, the Spanish officials were very much dismayed and annoyed. To them it appeared that the United States was trying to interfere. Unrest had quieted down, but if an American warship appeared in the harbor, it might again flare up. The Spanish government at Madrid felt exactly the same way about it, and although the Spanish premier in Madrid acquiesced in the move, because his minister in Washington had approved it, he did not like it a bit.

Within a few days the two warships were in Cuban waters; there was much relief when the officials of Havana gave the battleships a warm welcome. That night at a diplomatic dinner at the White House, Minister Dupuy de Lome was singled out by President McKinley for especially kind attention. All seemed well between the two nations.

Yet it almost seems that there was some decree of fate hanging over the two countries, for almost immediately came a disclosure which made Spanish-American relations worse than ever. A month before the White House dinner, Dupuy de Lome had written a letter to a friend in Havana in which he characterized McKinley as a cheap politician and made other unfriendly remarks about the United States and its President. The letter fell into the hands of the Cuban revolutionaries and they published it. The State Department asked the Spanish minister if he had written the letter. He said he had, and began packing his bags to go home. His usefulness was ended.

Then, as if planned, on the night of February 15 the "Maine" was ripped apart by an explosion, and 250 of her men died in the waters of Havana harbor.

Immediately a naval board of inquiry was convened to discover the cause of the explosion, and divers began searching the waters of the harbor for some clues. Was it accident or was it sabotage? That was the question to be decided.

For five long weeks the investigation continued, while the Hearst newspapers and other newspapers that wanted war fomented for it, and the American people wondered. The longer they waited the more the war spirit grew in the United States.

Attention was now focused on the United States navy and the public discovered what Theodore Roosevelt had been trying to say for several years, only to be squelched by his superiors: that the United States, with only seven modern armor-clad battleships, was not even a second rate naval power. The battleship "Oregon," one of the most modern of these, was not even available for service in the Atlantic, for it was on the Pacific coast. Orders were sent to the "Oregon" to steam around Cape Horn immediately. In Congress fifty million dollars was voted overnight to increase the United States navy's strength, and the naval procurement officers began ransacking shipyards all over the world to buy what vessels they could that might be quickly converted for use as warships. The voyage of the "Oregon" began, and here was another lesson: the Panama Canal must be built, and it must be controlled by the United States in the interests of her own defense.

As the investigation into the cause of the "Maine" disaster continued, American attitudes hardened. For several years the United States had demanded an end to the war in Cuba, which was fought primarily for reform in the beginning, but had become an insurrection as time went on.

McKinley decided the time had come for a showdown. He would demand that the war be ended without further delay by the Spanish government, no matter what terms of settlement must be achieved. A stiff note saying just this was sent to the Spanish government in Madrid. The Spanish premier realized that Spanish public opinion would not stand for such concessions as the Americans demanded. Minister Woodford knew this and told Washington so, but Washington was not listening. It was apparent that McKinley had made up his mind for war. So the Spanish government refused the American demands—for to accept them would have caused the fall of the cabinet, and perhaps even the fall of the kingdom, given a strong enough reaction at home. The situation had reached an impasse.

The Americans were now ready for war, and McKinley was committed to it if the Spanish did not back down. The newspapers, more aroused than ever by the preparations for war ordered by McKinley, began demanding revenge for the sinking of the "Maine."

On March 20 McKinley learned that the naval board of inquiry, still in Havana, was of the opinion that a naval mine, planted by unknown parties, had caused the destruction of the battleship, and when that news was made known to the public, the warmongers began to shout loudly, and the people began to respond with cries of war, having gotten used to the idea over a month's period.

McKinley then began consulting with members of Congress. He intended to demand full reparations from Spain for the destruction of the "Maine," but more important, to demand an immediate end to the struggle in Cuba. This meant that Spain would have to give up Cuba.

On March 25 the naval commission arrived from Havana with its report. It had found that the "Maine" suffered an external explosion on the port side which had caused the magazines to explode. (A Spanish naval commission, also examining the evidence, found that the "Maine" had blown up from some kind of internal explosion, but the Americans were not prepared to concede that the ship's destruction could have been an accident.) The findings were supposed to be secret, but the news leaked out somehow. On Monday, March 28, the Associated Press carried a story telling of the findings of the commission, and it was picked up by the newspapers all across the country.

McKinley said he was hoping for peace; but in the weeks that had passed since the sinking of the "Maine" he had not given the people any such guidance. But they heard much from the war party in Congress and from the war press.

Thus when President McKinley went before Congress with his message on the "Maine," it was too late to talk peace because all the country was talking war. The news of the ship's external destruction meant only one thing to Americans: that the United States had been attacked and had suffered a defeat. The demand for revenge swelled everywhere in America. The *New York Times* said editorially that there was no stopping the war unless Spain granted outright independence to Cuba.

It was possible that this might be done, for a diplomatic conference was to be held in Havana that week. Even as the war congressmen thundered for action on the floor of House and Senate, President McKinley waited for the results of that conference. Arrangements were made for the installation of a telegraph apparatus in the White House so the message could be transmitted direct from Minister Woodford as soon as the word was known. When the message came and was translated, it showed that the conference had produced too little, too late. The Spanish government was willing to make reforms in Cuba, but it was not willing to leave Cuba or even to call off the war against the insurgents through armistice.

McKinley did not want war. In the last few days of March he became drawn and haggard, worrying incessantly how he might avert the fighting. But it was too late, he had waited too long before making his feelings known to the public.

Even had he made his feelings known in February, perhaps he would have been unable to control the trend of American opinion. The immediate causes of the American surge of war feeling were the sinking of the "Maine" and the war of the insurgent Cubans against a harsh Spanish government in Cuba. But these were surface matters. Far beneath them lay the root causes of the American feeling; and these could be traced to a continuation of the policy of American expansion. All around the world the big powers were taking on colonies, and many Americans saw no reason that we should not do so too. Indeed, some Americans felt that it was disgraceful not to have our share and that the failure to own colonies marked us as an inferior power.

McKinley proposed to undertake what he hopefully called "neutral intervention"—without any conscious attempt at humor in the contradictory term.

Early in April he prepared a message to Congress. It was supposed to be delivered on April 6, but it was delayed when it became known that the Vatican and certain European powers wanted to intervene in the hope of preserving peace. The European powers were very much concerned about the possibility of war between the United States and Spain. It was hardly possible that the shattered and ineffectual government of Spain could win, and they feared that a victory of the United States would bring about the spread of Republican institutions across the world. (Remember that to the monarchies of Europe in the nineteenth century, the threat of a powerful and growing America was regarded in almost exactly the same terms as the democracies of Europe and America regarded the growing power of Soviet Russia in the twentieth century. The Europeans were eager to "contain" America, to use a twentieth-century term.)

The European efforts at intervention were successful in one sense. The Spanish government agreed to a cease-fire in Cuba. Unfortunately the agreement came too late, on the weekend of April 9 and 10; for by this time McKinley had lost control of Congress. Speaker Tom Reed announced to the press that he had lost control of the House of Representatives, and it was definitely known in Washington that if McKinley did not demand action during the following week, Congress was going to declare war.

When McKinley's recommendation for "neutral intervention" was received, Congress turned it into something quite different. Senator David Turpie of Indiana, a Democrat, proposed an amendment to the President's idea which would definitely recognize the insurgent government of Cuba. This meant war. The administration protested vigorously, because the President held that the Constitution gave him—not Congress—the power to carry on American relations with foreign lands and to recognize this government or that. The Turpie amendment to the resolution was finally stricken before it was passed.

All this took time. On April 20 McKinley finally signed the resolution calling for intervention to bring about order in Cuba, and an ultimatum was sent to Spain. The Spanish government, of course, rejected any attempt by the United States to interfere in Cuba. Diplomatic relations were broken off and, as of April 21, war began.

At this same time it became imperative that Secretary of State Sherman be replaced; for that week McKinley learned of a conversation the Secretary had held with the Austrian minister in which he had suffered a complete lapse of memory about American foreign policy. This could not go on. Sherman was told, and he resigned that weekend. He was replaced by William R. Day, who had been serving as an assistant in that department. It was a hectic time for the President. A blockade of Cuba was declared. Orders were sent to Commodore Dewey who headed the Asiatic navy squadron in Hong Kong, and he proceeded to sail to attack the Philippines. Then, on Monday, April 25, a formal declaration of war against Spain was made by Congress.

But making war—that was another matter. The United States, with a standing army limited by Congress to 25,000 men, was in no condition to make war on land. At sea, something was happening, but the nation was not quite sure what it was. On May 2 news came from Madrid by way of London that there had been a naval action in the Philippines the day before. The news report indicated that the Americans had won the fight. That was all that could be learned for a week, and during the week rumors took the place of facts. Soon the nation was worrying lest Commodore Dewey had lost the Asiatic fleet to the enemy.

On May 7 news finally came from Dewey, telling of an overwhelming victory in which the Spanish fleet was destroyed. Not one American life had been lost or one American ship sunk, and the American fleet controlled Manila Bay.

Then the war lagged, for no one was ready to fight except Dewey. Troops were needed to oppose the 10,000 man Spanish army in the Philippines, but they were not ready and there were no ships to transport them to the battle front.

The Spanish-American War was the greatest fiasco in which America had ever been involved. Neither War Department nor Navy Department was ready for action when war came. An invasion of Cuba was planned, but the military could not prepare for it. Still, the quartermaster corps prepared, and in the spring of 1898 enormous quantities of food were sent to Tampa, Florida, which was supposed to be the staging point for an army of 70,000 men. But the army did not exist; if it had existed, there was not enough ammunition on hand, and not enough could be manufactured in two months, to make it possible for such a force to fight. So a thousand boxcars loaded with food sat on the railroad sidings of the railroads of the South, waiting.

In a comedy of errors, Spain's western fleet was bottled up in Santiago harbor, and in June the United States finally sent an expeditionary force of 17,000 men to Cuba amid the most thorough confusion possible. Any movement by the enemy, any weather disturbance, would have been enough to imperil and perhaps wreck this amateur invasion force. But there was no enemy movement and there was no weather difficulty, and the ill-assorted group of miserable coastal steamers and gunboats made its way to the waters off Santiago, where the American fleet lay at anchor, guarding the Spaniards inside the bottled harbor. Among them was Lieutenant Colonel Theodore Roosevelt, who had resigned his post as Assistant Secretary of the Navy to command a unit of volunteer cavalry to be known later as the Rough Riders.

The naval warfare in the Caribbean was marked by pettiness and incompetence. Only because the incompetence of the Spanish fleet was the greater did the Americans win a signal victory at Santiago Bay, destroying the Spanish fleet without the loss of a single American ship.

The land war in Cuba continued for months, with thousands of Americans falling prey to the dreaded illnesses of malaria and yellow fever. The victory at Santiago occurred on July 3, 1898. Then came a victory at Wake Island. Beginning in July the Spanish opened negotiations for peace through the French ambassador in Washington. The terms were agreed upon, and plans were made for a formal treaty of peace to be negotiated at Paris in the autumn. The meetings began there in October, but much argument developed and the treaty was not signed until December 10. Under the treaty, the Spanish gave up Cuba, which became independent. As indemnity, or payment for the cost to America of

# CHAPTER 9

# World Power

THE END of the Spanish-American War did not resolve the problems of either Cuba or the Philippines. There was much disagreement as to what ought to be done with the latter islands. Over the conquests of this war, the country broke into two camps: the imperialists and the anti-imperialists. Generally speaking the imperialists were the Republicans; the anti-imperialists were the Democrats, the Populists, and a large number of Republicans of New England. The anti-imperialists took the position that the United States was, and should be, confined to the shores of North America and that foreign populations, which could not easily be assimilated into the American social structure, should not be brought into the American picture as possessions. This was the argument against accepting the Philippines as a colony, and indeed, against taking on the responsibility for Hawaii. The argument flared over two issues—the Hawaiian annexation treaty, which had been considered while the Spanish-American War was in progress, and the Paris treaty with Spain. In the end, Hawaii was annexed and the Treaty of Paris was accepted when Democrats, led by William Jennings Bryan, took the position that at least the treaty would put an end to the imperialist war. The matter of colonies was settled when General Aguinaldo, commander of the Philippine insurrectionists, broke with the Americans and engaged in battle with them on the island of Luzon. Now a terrible mess had developed. The United States had assumed de facto responsibility for the governing of the Philippines and the Spanish government had disintegrated. With Aguinaldo carrying on warfare against the Americans, there was no time for temporizing. American lives were being lost as the Senate argued, and this could not be permitted. The Treaty of Paris was carried to passage on the guns of Aguinaldo. Regular army troops were sent to the Philippines to replace the volunteers who had fought against Spain. The struggle to bring about peace in the Philippines lasted another three years, although organized resistance ended in 1899 and Aguinaldo was captured in 1901. Then came the long task, carried out by a succession of other administrations, to prepare the Philippines for independence.

By the beginning of 1899, then, the United States was very much an imperialist nation, although the population of the country was divided on its attitudes toward possession of colonies and would be so for many years. Still the colonies existed and they must be policed and guided; and this involved the establishment of new arms of government and a new policy. The problem was to determine how the people of the new territories should be treated. Always before, American territorial acquisition had been on the North American continent, and the people had been of the same stock as those in Pennsylvania or Massachusetts or Georgia. Now, suddenly, the United States' new territories included Filipinos, Malays, Chinese, Japanese, Hawaiians and other Polynesians, and people of Spanish and Indian descent in the southern Caribbean. Should all these people have full citizenship? How should these new colonies be governed—or should they govern themselves? All these questions were new but they had to be faced immediately because there could be no vacuum of government.

It would have been simple enough if the administration had declared that the constitutional rights of Americans extended to all these people who lived under the American flag. But in the nineteenth century, Americans were not ready to admit the equality of mankind. After considerable debate, Cuba was granted the independence promised her (once she fell into American hands a group of imperialists tried to turn Cuba into an American colony). Puerto Rico was treated as a colony, with no self-government but an appointed governor and appointed legislators. The problem of the Philippines occupied much of the time of the State and War Departments, and the President, but it was not to be resolved during McKinley's lifetime. The fighting continued in the islands as the insurgents struggled for complete independence, not really believing that the United States ever intended to give them freedom, and determined not to exchange a Spanish master for an American master. In his 1899 annual message to Congress, after struggling with the problem for months, the President recommended that legislation regarding the future of the Philippines be deferred until the rebellion was suppressed, and that is how it was left. A special Philippine Commission submitted a report of four large volumes that recommended a scheme of civil government. But it also recommended that until the rebellion was over, the plan should be put in the hands of the President for execution as he saw fit.

It was generally assumed in 1899 that McKinley would be a candidate to succeed himself in office the following year—by nearly everyone except McKinley. One night in the White House when he was visiting with Republican leaders he realized that they were talking as if his renomination were an accepted fact. He spoke up, "If what you gentlemen are saying implies that I am a candidate for renomination next year, I want to say to you that I would be the happiest man in America if I could go out of office in 1901, of course with the feeling that I had reasonably met the expectations of the people. I have had enough of it, Heaven knows! I have had all the honor there is in the place and responsibilities enough to kill any man. . . . There is only one condition upon which I would listen to such a suggestion, and that is, a perfectly clear and imperative call to duty. . . ."

McKinley meant what he said. He was seriously worried about the condition of his wife, who was not bearing up at all well under the responsibilities of the White House. She was surrounded by friends and relatives who kept from the general public the fact that she was an epileptic; but seizures did begin without notice, and occasionally one began when strangers were in the house. Then the members of the household quietly removed her or escorted the strangers away, noting that Mrs. McKinley was not well and tired easily. A few people in Washington knew about her disease, but not so many as one might think, because in those days it was not considered polite to inquire into the illnesses of a lady.

And yet William McKinley was not being totally honest with himself or his listeners when he argued about the "call to duty." He would hear the call to duty if he wished, for there were always loyal Republicans to make it; and he realized that he had now started a policy in America that was different from anything that went before and that it must be guarded lest it be lost. His policy called for colonialism—enlightened colonialism, but still colonialism—for extension of American business activity all around the world, and for increased American interest and involvement in world affairs. Until this time the United States had never regarded itself as a part of any community of nations.

Americans harked back, always, to the policies enunciated by George Washington against foreign entanglements; and they had modified these only insofar as the Monroe Doctrine was concerned in protection of American interests in the western hemisphere, and the increase in American trade in the Far East. McKinley had done more than any other man to end that American isolation from world affairs, and he recognized this. He was willing to accept the responsibilities that went with the emergence of the United States as a world power, but he felt the need to instruct his party and his people in those responsibilities.

During his first term, McKinley also suffered serious social problems and stupidities in the White House. Since Mrs. McKinley was so unwell, she could not take over the duties of social secretary, as many other First Ladies had done. Instead, McKinley was surrounded by sycophants who wished to make the White House a pinnacle of American social activity. Two White House aides, Addison Porter and Captain Theodore Bingham, set themselves up as arbiters of everything, including fashions. The problem was further complicated by Admiral Dewey and other naval officers who, feeling that they were the heroes of the war against Spain, attempted to outmaneuver the army generals on the field of protocol. Who was to go first into a White House reception—this was the kind of question that upset these small minds and kept Washington society humming in the winter of 1899. McKinley finally put an end to it when he saw an article in the Washington *Evening Star* ordering ladies who came to the White House not to wear bonnets. He grew so angry that he prepared a statement of his own for the *Star*, saying he did not care what the ladies wore. He was persuaded not to send the statement (which would have ruined his staff), but after it was written there was no more snob trouble.

Apparently, matters could not be better for the Republi-

can party than they were in the winter of 1899-1900. The
Fifty-sixth Congress was quiet, from the Republican point
of view, because for the first time since 1883 the Republicans controlled both houses and the White House at the
same time. The Silver Bloc was much shrunk and did not
seem to offer much danger. Speaker Tom Reed of the House
of Representatives, who detested the new policy of imperialism and fought it all the way, had retired from
politics.

Yet all was not as well as it seemed, because the Democrats were determined to be as vengeful in opposing administration legislation as was possible. The Democrats in
this session were divided among themselves, between free
silver and hard money men, and in their impotence there
was only one agreement they could make—to fight against
anything the Republican majority wished, or any piece of
legislation backed by the President. One of the first pieces
of legislation they opposed was a bill which would give the
President the power to administer civil government in the
Philippines. Even as that bill was being considered, McKinley was thinking about whom to appoint to head the civil
commission. He finally settled on Judge William Howard
Taft of Cincinnati, a big, bluff man who was far more
lawyer than politician and whose real ambition in life was
to secure a seat on the United States Supreme Court.

McKinley called Judge Taft to Washington without telling him why. The Judge knew there was no Supreme Court
post open at the moment, and he was puzzled. When he arrived at the White House, McKinley said he would like to
have the Judge go to the Philippines, perhaps to head up
this civilian commission.

Taft later reported part of the conversation:

"I said, 'Mr. President, what do you mean by going to
the Philippines?'

"He replied, 'We must establish a government there and I would like you to help.'

"I said, 'I am sorry we have got the Philippines. I don't want them and I think you ought to have some man who is more in sympathy with the situation.'

" 'You don't want them any less than I do,' replied the President, 'but we have got them and in dealing with them I think I can trust the man who didn't want them better than I can the man who did.' "

So Taft took the post. "I went under the influence of Mr. McKinley's personality," he said later, "the influence he had of making people do what they ought to do in the interest of the public service."

Among the Republicans the imperialists had grown strong. McKinley now took some pains to disassociate himself from this group, and to assure the nation that there would be no general campaign of territorial aggrandizement. What he was saying was that the imperialism of the United States had gone about as far as it was going to go; that since we had taken on these foreign possessions we were beginning, as a nation, to have some very serious doubts about the wisdom of the course and to wonder what these possessions would do to the American economy.

This problem so troubled the high-tariff men that they introduced a measure which provided for taxation of goods that were imported from Puerto Rico, a United States possession. Here was a serious moral problem for the nation, and one that William McKinley met badly in a moral way.

The original thirteen colonies had been driven to revolt from the mother government of England because of taxation without representation. Now, in 1900, the Republican party in power in Congress and the White House chose to behave in the same way that the English Parliament had behaved in the middle of the eighteenth century. McKinley, who at first recommended free trade with Puerto Rico, reversed himself when this was put to him in terms of the tariff (for he was always a protective tariff man), and he came out for taxation without representation of this American possession. His intervention then made it possible for the Republicans to pass the bill.

This unfair measure lost much popularity for the Republicans. Many Republican newspapers came out in favor of freedom—"the Constitution follows the flag" was a favorite pronouncement at this time. It was a slap at those who would abandon constitutional principles when it came to economic interests.

McKinley explained his reasons for his course privately, although not publicly. He said he saw a need for asserting the right of Congress to govern the colonies with a "free hand," particularly when the Democrats had held that the Constitution automatically extended to the islands. In other words, in order to keep the Constitution from being extended, he had backed this unfair legislation. But he had not even backed it publicly. Instead he had done what he had done many times before when faced with a difficult issue—he had been less than frank and had chosen silence, which was the least harmful to him politically, if it was also the most damaging to his reputation as statesman when it came to the judgment of history. He had also sacrificed the strong popularity he had with the people at the end of the war; for the people, if not the politicians, favored the extension of the United States Constitution to cover all men who lived in American territory.

The truth was that McKinley had made his change of policy in order to assure party unity. In her study, *In The Days of McKinley*, Margaret Leech noted that "this most beloved of Presidents had failed to meet the test of greatness." Even more, in 1900, the Republican party, which had been organized as a revolutionary party to bring about the equality of the Negro in America, was turning from radical to ultra-conservative. In this battle over the tariff for Puerto Rico the ultra-conservatives won the day. In a sense, one might say that until 1900, no matter how vindictive the Republicans had been in the Reconstruction of the South, the party had retained its identity as the party of freedom, opposed to restraints on any of the people. Now came this change—the greatest blow ever struck against the revolutionary principles on which the American government had been founded more than a century before.

Even while the McKinley administration was quietly overturning the American Revolution's greatest accomplishment—the theory of equality of all under the law—in international affairs the same administration was showing a degree of statesmanship hitherto unmatched in American affairs.

In 1898 the British government had opened discussion with the United States about guarantees for equal commercial opportunity of the nationals of both countries in the China trade. The American government had rejected these ideas as contrary to the American policy of non-involvement in the affairs of other nations. That attitude was recognized as an extremely foolish one a few months later, in view of American involvement in Cuba and the Philippines, and the policy was modified. It became apparent to the State Department that the big foreign powers were moving rapidly into China and that unless something was done they would soon control all trade along this huge Asian coast.

What is called the Open Door policy of the United States toward China was the result. It was actually devised by an Englishman named Alfred E. Hippisley, who had served in the Chinese customs office for a number of years. Hippisley was an advisor to McKinley's third Secretary of State, John Hay, and he drafted a memorandum pointing out that China was in danger of being broken up into little colonies. He offered a remedy, and this was the Open Door endorsed by John Hay and accepted by McKinley.

The Open Door policy provided that each European power would guarantee to stop interfering with any treaty port (port occupied by treaty) or existing interest of any other power in China. The second guarantee was that the Chinese tariff treaty then in force with all these nations would remain in force and would apply to these spheres of influence. Taxes on trade would be collected by the Chinese government. The third provision was that no power would discriminate against others in favor of its own citizens regarding railroad charges and harbor fees.

It was easy, in reading this, to see what was happening in China. The Russians, Germans, English, and French were seizing control of certain areas. In each area they developed the harbors and the railroads. Then they discriminated against foreigners in these areas, so that their nationals would have the best of it in trade. They also threatened to destroy what was left of the central government of China in Peking by taking away China's right to collect taxes all over the country. Soon, if nothing was done, China would cease to exist as a nation.

Secretary Hay instructed the United States embassies in Berlin, St. Petersburg, London, Paris, Rome, and Tokyo to take copies of this memorandum to the foreign offices and demand assurances that the governments involved would adhere to this policy. The governments of the European nations and Japan issued evasive replies, but Hay would have none of it. He announced that each government had agreed to accept the Open Door policy, it was

now "final and definitive," and that the United States would
set about making sure that this would be so.

The need to have the battleship "Oregon" sail around
Cape Horn during the Spanish-American War's opening
days was not lost on the American people, on Congress, or
on the McKinley administration. As the war opened against
Spain, John Hay began to work for the building of a
Panama canal by the United States alone.

The first problem was to settle long-standing differences
with Great Britain. Under the Clayton-Bulwer Treaty of
1850 neither United States nor Britain could build a canal
without the cooperation and concurrence of the other nation. The result of that treaty was that for forty years no
canal had been built. Most recently the French had tried to
build a canal, but their effort had failed.

In 1898 negotiations with the British were begun, and an
American canal commission set to work to find the best
location for an isthmian crossing. Soon the treaty, called
the Hay-Pauncefote treaty, was agreed upon and signed.
It ran into serious opposition in Congress in 1900, because
this was an election year, and because the United States had
agreed not to fortify the canal. But the Hay-Pauncefote
treaty was not to be ratified by the Senate that year. Rather
than have it defeated, McKinley agreed with his leaders in
Congress that it be held over until the next session, after the
elections.

The treaty was important, but there were more important matters at hand. While those negotiations had been
going on, there had been difficulties in China. In 1898,
while the Open Door was being examined, a revolutionary
group of Chinese known as the Boxers had risen against
foreign interference in China, and for a time it appeared
that China must be the scene of a serious conflict. In the

end, however, the Chinese government collapsed before the opposition of the European powers, and the United States sent troops, too, to protect its interests. The Chinese capital at Peking was occupied and the government was forced into many concessions to the foreigners. One saving factor was the Open Door policy announced by America. Had it not been for this policy China might actually have been cut up into foreign colonies. But with the Americans holding out, the other westerners and the Japanese and Russians agreed to settle for less than total colonization of the Chinese kingdom.

# CHAPTER 10

# The Election of 1900

WELL BEFORE THE END of McKinley's first term in office, Vice-President Garret Hobart had died. In 1900 there was very little question in anyone's mind as to who the next Republican nominee would be; the one vital question was who would be the vice-presidential candidate.

There were half a dozen candidates for the post, most of them Republican leaders in the Senate or the House of Representatives. There was one man in the country who did not want the post, and who came to Washington in June, 1900, to announce that he did not want it and to deny that he would be persuaded to be a candidate for the job.

This man was Theodore Roosevelt. There was good reason for his trip to Washington, because Tom Platt, the Republican boss of New York State, was doing his best to push Teddy Roosevelt into the vice-presidency. The idea was to kick Roosevelt upstairs, to get him out of the governorship of New York which he had occupied for the past two years. There were several reasons for this and, in the manner of machine party politics, they were extremely complicated. It is enough to say that Platt would feel more secure as party boss if Teddy Roosevelt were in Washington, and Platt also had some scores to settle with the McKinley backers, who he felt had attempted to interfere in his bailiwick.

The Republican leaders of the McKinley administration were not completely aware of Tom Platt's stubbornness and power. When Roosevelt arrived in Washington to announce that he really did not want the vice-presidency, they did not pay much attention to him, except to agree genially that he ought to stay in New York and run for governor again. McKinley was friendly about it, but preoccupied with the China and Panama problems. Mark Hanna was brutal: "You're not fit for it," he said. John Hay was amused. Roosevelt discovered that nobody in the administration took him seriously, that nobody had paid any attention to Tom Platt's ideas.

If the Republican leaders in Washington had known their man better, they would not have treated him in so offhand a fashion. One of Teddy Roosevelt's salient qualities was an insistence on being taken seriously, no matter how boyish he might seem to others. In a way, Hanna and Hay and the others played directly into Tom Platt's hands when they laughed at Roosevelt's position. By so doing they made the vice-presidency more attractive to him, by far, than it had been before—if only because it now seemed that it might be hard to get.

But Teddy Roosevelt still did not want the job, and he went back to Albany saying just that. This disappointed many of his friends, because he had come out of the Spanish-American War as one of its heroes, and his name was well known and loved across the country; he had the unusual advantage of an easterner who was well loved even in the West.

Until McKinley's day the vice-presidency had been a political prison. The Vice-President, elected by the people, had no duties except to preside over the Senate, where he might vote in case of ties, and to succeed the President in case of the latter's death. So the vice-presidency was what the President would make of it. Until McKinley's time no President had made much of it since Jackson quarreled with John C. Calhoun, when they were President and Vice-President respectively. It was generally accepted that the vice-presidential nomination was given to an old party wheelhorse, preferably from some weak or questionable state where party power needed shoring up. The governorship of nearly any state was regarded as a much surer stepping stone to the presidency; so was the Senate of the United States, or the House of Representatives, or a generalship in the army in time of war.

William McKinley, however, had made something more of the vice-presidency than other Presidents. He had been genuinely fond of Hobart and had given Hobart many responsibilities within the administration, principally those of an advisor whose advice was sought and weighed carefully.

Teddy Roosevelt really wanted to run for governor of New York for another two-year term or to be appointed to the McKinley cabinet. Roosevelt's most important supporter in Congress, Senator Henry Cabot Lodge, wanted Roosevelt to take the vice-presidency, because he thought it would be a good post for him. Lodge spoke to McKinley about this, and the President said he had absolutely no objections to Roosevelt. So Lodge told Teddy Roosevelt he would have to make up his mind.

Meanwhile, in Albany, Teddy Roosevelt had learned that Platt was eager to have him out of New York for his own reasons, and this made Roosevelt angry and as terribly, terribly stubborn as he could get. He made a public statement that he would not, under any circumstances, accept the Republican nomination for Vice-President.

McKinley was of two minds. He had rather liked Roosevelt when they had met in Washington in the early days of
the administration (when Roosevelt was Assistant Secretary
of the Navy). McKinley detested political "deals," however,
and he knew the men involved: Platt, and Matthew Quay,
the powerful Republican boss of Pennsylvania. If the delegates to the Republican national convention really wanted
Roosevelt, he would be pleased enough. It was only if the
bosses were pushing him that McKinley would object.

In that spring of 1900, McKinley was very worried about
what to do with Mark Hanna. Hanna was both an asset and
a liability. He was an asset because he was so adept at organ-
izing and so completely loyal to McKinley. He was a liability because he was a machine politician. At that time
there was a considerable aversion to machine politicians
throughout America, and McKinley, who had watched the
struggle of machine politicians in Ohio for twenty years,
had no use for this kind of politics as a matter of principle.
He struggled with the problem, and wondered whether or
not he might best find another chairman for the Republican National Committee. In the end, however, he retained
Hanna.

The Republican National Convention was held in Philadelphia in 1900. Strangely enough, Theodore Roosevelt
was there as a delegate-at-large from New York, although
Senator Lodge had told him to stay away from the convention if he did not wish to be nominated for the vice-presidency. Lodge knew that Teddy Roosevelt was the most in-
teresting character at the convention. (McKinley would not
be there because it was not considered proper for a candidate to attend the convention.) The newspapermen were
sure to be watching Roosevelt and writing about his every
action. In a characteristic display, Teddy appeared in his
old Rough Rider hat, which gave them even more to talk
about.

Hanna was very much opposed to Roosevelt's nomination and he did everything he could to stop it. Once, in a heated argument, he made a rash statement: "Don't any of you realize that there's only one life between that madman and the presidency?" But McKinley would not allow Hanna to use the President's power to dictate that Roosevelt be ruled out. The more Hanna worked against Roosevelt, the faster Roosevelt's mind was changed and his enthusiasm for the vice-presidency aroused. Roosevelt had only one more question in his mind as the convention began: how did McKinley feel about it? He sent his friend George Perkins to Washington. Perkins conferred with George Cortelyou, McKinley's secretary, and came back to Philadelphia with the news that McKinley was very friendly to him and that he would, if elected, occupy the same important role in the new administration that Hobart had in the last. Roosevelt was convinced. He won and accepted the Republican nomination for Vice-President.

All this argument had detracted somewhat from the issues at the convention. The Republican platform was left full of holes, and the Democrats, who met in Kansas City a few weeks later, made up a platform that called attention to these deficiencies. There was only one thing to be done to repair the oversights, and there was only one man to do it: McKinley must make a major political address outlining Republican policies and answering Democratic criticisms.

He chose to do so from the porch of the house on North Market Street in Canton. He and Ida came home from Washington and were met there by Senator Lodge, the chairman of the Republican party's notification committee. Then the President accepted the Republican nomination again and replied to the Democrats. Again William Jennings Bryan would be the Democratic candidate and again Bryan would fight for free silver. As in the past McKinley accepted this as the most important issue before the country. He talked about the Open Door, and about the Panama Canal, the tariff and prosperity, and he stated that the war must be ended and peace brought to the Philippines, whereupon a just government would be installed there.

So the campaign began. It was not to be nearly so serious a problem for the Republicans to win the election in 1900 as it had been in 1896. Mark Hanna thought it would be relatively simple. He would direct the campaign along the lines that would be most effective: the Republicans would show how they were bringing prosperity to the nation and how the Democrats had lost it, and how the Democrats would destroy the country with their cheap money if they were allowed to take power. There were some problems— the continued fighting in the Philippines and the lack of effort made by the McKinley administration to control the business trusts. McKinley had told the people that he was going to control the trusts in his first administration, but he had not done so.

In this campaign Hanna and McKinley nearly quarrelled. Hanna had become very crotchety. He was sixty-two years old, a tired, sick, and lame man. He was nervous about his own position in the Republican party, and he sensed that McKinley did not have the same trust in him that he had once had. The reason was that McKinley, as a man of high purpose and principle, abhorred many of the moves that Hanna took to retain Republican power.

The argument arose, finally, over a decision by Hanna to make a speaking tour of the Populist and Democratic areas of the country. Many of Hanna's friends felt that he could only hurt the Republican cause by going to these areas, particularly to Nebraska and South Dakota, which were strong Bryan areas. Hanna insisted that he would go, and he made arrangements for the tour.

Postmaster-General Charles E. Smith was sent to Chicago, where Hanna was running the campaign, with a message from Washington. The cabinet was worried about Hanna's activities, and McKinley was concerned too. Hanna had made some rash statements about Republican policy—for example, denying that trusts existed when everyone knew they were much alive and that the President had even sent a message to Congress about trust regulation a year or so before.

When Smith walked into Republican headquarters and expressed concern over Hanna's proposed trip, Hanna lost his temper. He sent Smith back to Washington with the message that "God hates a coward," which indicated that he was going to continue with his trip and his efforts, in his own way, to win the election.

The breach was healed not long after when Hanna met McKinley for luncheon in Canton, and Hanna was allowed to go on his trip, during which he was careful with his statements and made a good impression. But the Hanna and McKinley relationship was never the same again after that first term and the struggle in the convention over the nomination of Roosevelt.

Even Hanna agreed before the campaign was over that Roosevelt was helpful to the ticket. Hanna sent him on the stump, to follow Bryan's campaign in the Middle West, where Bryan was strong, and to make his intensely nationalist feelings known where they would do the most good.

One of the serious worries of the campaign of 1900 was for the safety of the President during the excitement of election year. Within four years, three important world figures had been assassinated by anarchists: the Empress Elizabeth of Austria, President Carnot of France, and the Spanish premier. In 1898 a special secret service guard had been established to protect the President; but when the war ended these precautions had been cut down, and in 1900 only a single guard was assigned to the White House. In that summer of 1900, Mark Hanna heard of a plot by anarchists to assassinate a number of rulers and political leaders, among them the King of Italy, the Czar of Russia, and the President of the United States. On July 29 King Humbert of Italy was killed by an assassin who had been until then employed at a silk factory in Paterson, New Jersey. Hanna and others had good reason to fear that the center of the anarchists was in the United States. A full-time guard was assigned to the President, but he could not function very effectively because William McKinley was indifferent to the dangers he might face. He believed that they were highly overstated, and he would not allow the guard to accompany him on drives that he took with Ida around Washington. He often gave his bodyguard the slip as he went out for a stroll by himself in the evening. In Canton he insisted on living the life of a private citizen when he walked down to the business district, stopping to talk to old friends, or when he went to church. He did not forget that he was President of the United States, but neither did he forget that it was an elective office and that he was President by the will of the people. When the election returns of November, 1900, come in, he was even more sobered and impressed than he had been in 1896, for the responsibility was greater than ever. The American people had elected him by the largest majority won by a Republican since 1872.

# CHAPTER 11

# The Second Term

THE WILLIAM MCKINLEY who faced his second term as President was a far more thoughtful and impressive figure than he had been four years before, when the novelty of holding the highest office in the land had impressed him as much as the responsibility that went with it. Now his single concern was for the responsibility: he wanted to see to a positive conclusion the major policies that had been developed in his first administration. He wanted a decent government for the Philippines and for every other American possession, whether acquired in the Spanish war or otherwise. He wanted the canal built across the isthmus of Panama. He wanted the principle of arbitration of international differences to be established among nations, and he truly believed this could be done so that war would be forever outlawed. He wanted a reasonable settlement of the damages American property had suffered in the Boxer Rebellion in China, on the principle that the long-range friendship between the two countries could not be increased by a harsh settlement and must be assisted by a merciful one. He wanted treaties of reciprocity with other nations to lessen harmful competition of industries and make it easier for trade to be increased.

All these policies had their roots in his administration,

which was the most enlightened in many a year in the matter of foreign affairs. Events had made it so; Grover Cleveland was not stupid or too stubborn to conduct a reasonable foreign policy, but in his day the seeds of imperialism had not grown so rapidly that a whole new face must be turned to foreign affairs. McKinley was the first President to realize that America's position among nations demanded an entirely new outlook in her foreign affairs.

During the political campaign McKinley had been outraged at the conduct of William Jennings Bryan and his associates. It was a fierce campaign. Bryan believed that he could win only if he was able to tarnish the reputation of the administration sufficiently, and he certainly tried to do that. He referred to the "invertebrate"—meaning McKinley—and charged the administration with betraying the ten commandments of Christ and of behaving like a crowned king. Bryan made an attempt to walk off with the McKinley moral program, and he said McKinley was deluding the people of the Philippines and the other former Spanish colonies with false promises that he never intended to keep.

Once the election was over, however, McKinley simmered down immediately and he refused to allow his subordinates to carry on the arguments that had been raised. Quite properly he decided that the victorious need not answer the defeated or impose upon them, and he returned to his consideration of national problems as if the election had not been held.

Mrs. McKinley's epilepsy was a serious burden for the President always. She insisted on playing the role of First Lady, which meant that she and those around her must make an heroic effort for every public occasion, and even then she might lose consciousness at any moment. Even "at home" there was no absolute protection against the attacks. One night while playing bridge with friends in the

White House, Ida McKinley suffered an attack and lost consciousness. McKinley quickly dropped a handkerchief over her face to shield the others from the sight of rolling eyes and slavering lips, and played a card from her hand. In a moment the attack ended, and Mrs. McKinley's one remark was, "Who played that card for me?"

It was a difficult problem for McKinley, and yet he never complained. His one heartfelt lament was made to the wife of his first Vice-President. "Oh, if you could have seen what a beauty Ida was as a girl," he had once said to Mrs. Hobart.

In Washington, McKinley was known for many qualities of his personality, and he was a very popular President among Washingtonians, whose standards for popularity are far more personal than those of the nation at large. He was known to love children; neither of his children lived to adulthood, and McKinley spent much time with the children at the Sunday school of his church. On the days of his public receptions Republican women came to call with their children, and the East Room was usually swarming with youngsters on these occasions. He was one of the champion baby-kissers of all times, and on visiting days some lucky child always walked off with the bright pink carnation that the President wore each day. Once when Mrs. Cortelyou, the wife of his secretary, came to call with her two sons, McKinley gave one boy the carnation from his buttonhole and then picked another carnation from a vase, wore it for a moment, and handed it to the other boy so neither could have an advantage.

Each presidential family made some mark on the White House, and the McKinley mark was the love of flowers. On the west side of the mansion were located the conservatories and hothouses, where the McKinleys spent much time. Their rooms and the President's office were always filled with fresh flowers.

The new year 1901 began in some confusion at the White House. The President contracted a cold and it grew serious, finally developing into influenza. His doctors came and the President was confined to bed, a fact that was kept from the press and the public. It was possible to do so in those days, because there was not the invasion of the President's private life that future chief executives would suffer. Mr. McKinley could be in bed for a week. Only if he missed too many public appointments, too many receptions in the East Room, would lips begin to murmur that something was wrong. Fortunately in this one serious illness while he occupied the White House, McKinley recovered without the complication of pneumonia. His strength returned rather slowly, and he cancelled some official appointments and social invitations, including two cabinet meetings. But by January 22 the President was fit again and the first cabinet meeting of the new year was held.

There were serious problems to be faced. McKinley had asked for a reorganization of the army, seeing the need in the bumbling that had occurred during the Spanish-American War. Congress had investigated and drawn up some legislation, but the army officers' corps had managed to wreck the reforms—or so it seemed. The President and his Secretary of War, Elihu Root, told Congress that they must make the necessary reforms or face a special session of Congress. Also, Congress had become so deeply involved in "pork-barrel" and "logrolling" legislation that the River and Harbor Bill, which was to provide for public improvements, was becoming a monstrosity. President McKinley told Secretary Cortelyou that if Congress sent him a bad bill he would veto it without question—and that word was passed on to the Senate where the laws were under consideration.

There were problems in the Philippines, where Commissioner Taft reported that it was most difficult for the civilian government to rule under the laws passed by Congress and asked for some reforms. In Cuba, where the constitutional commission was meeting to draw up a plan for self-government, there were also difficulties, and those in charge indicated that they would not pay too much attention to the President's ideas.

Altogether, the President was not pleased with the accomplishments of this Congress and had let it be known several times that he was considering calling a special session. This idea did not appeal at all to the congressmen. It was already January. They would normally adjourn on March 4, inauguration day, and then head back to their constituencies to mend fences and make new friends until December when Congress met again. Nine months seems a long time to be spending away from the major job, but travel was not so easy or fast in the United States, and the pace of life was more leisurely. The break of a special session would create difficulties and annoyances for many members of Congress.

The problem of Cuba was a knotty one and was causing some delay. McKinley and Congress had agreed to treat Cuba as a foreign country, but the administration also wanted it to be said plainly that the United States would maintain a "protective interest" in the affairs of Cuba. In the United States Senate some members wanted to do what the President wished. Others wondered how the United States could claim the right to regulate any relations with a foreign country. (The basic unreasonableness of the McKinley position was to make itself felt nearly sixty years later.) Yet the President was determined that Congress should accept a special position for Cuba in American affairs, over and above that of all the hemisphere as covered by the Monroe Doctrine. Unless Congress did so, he assured his friends, there would most definitely be an extra session.

Congress accepted the President's bullying in its desire to get away from Washington. As far as the Philippines was concerned it did not work out as well as McKinley wished —he did not get the outright changes in the law that he had asked and Taft had wanted. But much of the difficulty in the Philippines was ironed out when Taft was appointed civilian governor of the islands, and General Arthur Mac-Arthur was relieved of command there. MacArthur was a military man of the old stripe, and he would not brook civilian interference. He and Taft did not quarrel only because Taft held his temper, or at least concealed his anger at the treatment he received from the General. (Later this treatment caused General MacArthur to lose the chief command of the army, when Taft became President.)

In the end, to try to meet the President's wishes and get away from Washington, Congress sat all night on March 3, passing four appropriations bills but not accepting the Rivers and Harbors Bill at all; it was subjected to a fili-buster which ended just in time for Vice-President Roose-velt to be sworn in, without delaying the inaugural cere-monies on March 4.

In his second inaugural speech, the President spoke briefly of the prosperity America enjoyed, the larger foreign markets that were now being sought in the new approach to foreign relations, and the responsibilities that America must assume among nations. He talked of the need for peaceful arbitration, underlining his hopes that the Hague peace convention would become the ruling force of nations, replacing war. He asked that Americans join in remember-ing the great principles of the Republic as laid down by the founding fathers, not at all conscious that he had lost his chance for greatness by refusing to back the principle of constitutional rights for every person who lived under the American flag.

CHAPTER 12

# The Swing Around the Nation

PRESIDENT MCKINLEY was fairly well pleased with the accomplishments of Congress when it adjourned, and he felt it possible to make the national tour that he had been planning since his second election. The plan called for him to leave Washington at the end of April and go to the Pacific coast by the southern rail route, then come back by the northern route. In San Francisco he would preside at the launching of the new battleship "Ohio," which represented the growth in America's naval might and an entirely new approach to naval affairs. The trip would end with a special President's Day at the Pan-American Exposition in Buffalo, New York.

There was a reason for the tour, and it had very little to do with partisan politics. The President was not totally pleased with the situation he found within his own party. Although the upcoming Fifty-seventh Congress would contain 55 Republicans in the Senate, as opposed to 35 Democrats and Populists, and 197 Republicans in the House, as opposed to 151 Democrats and 9 Fusionists—third party members—McKinley felt that he needed the public's support for two major areas of legislation in which Congress was dragging its feet in spite of presidential urgings.

First was the control of trusts. Second was the extension

of reciprocal trade. McKinley favored the high tariff for protection, but only if reciprocal trade could not be arranged. This was a development in his attitude which had been most notable since he had come to the presidency and had been faced with the problems of administering a trade program in the interests of all the nation, and not just the manufacturing regions. In Congress no one spoke much against the principle of reciprocal trade—it was hard to take a stand against so good an idea—but when it came to voting, the specific changes needed to put such a program into effect were always defeated. The President had submitted seven commercial treaties to the Fifty-sixth Congress and not one of them had been passed. The worst enemy of these treaties, strangely enough, was the man who had once had great influence with President McKinley— Senator Mark Hanna.

Hanna was also an implacable enemy of the regulation of the trusts. As a millionaire manufacturer in his own right, he believed stoutly in the power of capital and would do nothing, in trade or business regulation, to impinge on that power.

On his tour the President proposed to talk about the trusts; but his major effort would be made on the more simple and stirring issue of the seven treaties that sat, useless, in the box of the United States Senate Foreign Relations Committee.

On the morning of April 29, 1901, President McKinley and a party of more than forty persons left Washington on a special train bound for the West. On the train were officials of his administration, members of his staff, newspaper reporters, servants, and the President's secret service agent —the special guard assigned to protect him at all times. There were only two cabinet officials on the tour, because the others were very busy with their official business in Washington. The two were Secretary Hay, who came along since he was vitally concerned with the tariff matters and reciprocal trade, and Postmaster-General Smith.

The presidential party arrived in Los Angeles during the second week of May, and McKinley was drawn through the streets of that city in a carriage pulled by six white horses, leading a huge floral parade. After several speeches and several days of relaxation in the warm sun, the party left for a weekend in the resort city of Del Monte. McKinley made more speeches. Mrs. McKinley, who was suffering from a bone growth on her finger which had become inflamed, was not able to participate in all the festivities. She grew quite ill with fever, and the party cut short its visit to Del Monte and moved on to San Francisco so she could rest in bed for several days. There she developed a blood infection that became very serious. A group of doctors were called, with a new set of medications and treatments, and she recovered.

Mrs. McKinley was much sicker than most of the people around her knew, and the President sensed this, even as he went to the Union Iron Works to launch the new navy ship, the "Ohio." He was much distressed because he had to cross the bay, and during the crossings by ferry he was out of telegraphic communication with the house where his wife was so ill. For a time she was unconscious, but she responded to heart stimulants and came back quickly. Even so, much of the official program was cancelled, including several dinners and public speeches, much to the disappointment of the people of San Francisco. As it turned out, McKinley did not make a single one of the important speeches on national policy that he had planned so well. His wife's illness put the thought of them out of his mind.

Oddly enough, it did not matter. The press reported fully on Ida's illness, and the nation responded with a great wave of sympathy. Fathers, mothers, and children everywhere understood how great was the President's worry over his wife, and this concern touched them deeply. By the time Ida McKinley was recovering in San Francisco and the plans were made to move on for the next leg of the trip, President McKinley's personal popularity hit an all-time high. He returned to Washington with the party, cheers ringing on every side.

At this time, the President's growing popularity became a matter of concern, because there was developing even in this first year of his second term a considerable amount of talk about a third term. This idea was most repugnant to McKinley, and yet he did not know quite what to do about it. Eventually, on the night of June 10, he called a special meeting of the cabinet. Then, after consulting with his advisors, he issued a statement to the press.

"I will say now, once for all, expressing a long-settled conviction, that I not only am not and will not be a candidate for a third term, but would not accept a nomination for it if it were tendered me. My only ambition is to serve through my second term to the acceptance of my countrymen, whose generous confidence I so deeply appreciate, and then with them to do my duty in the ranks of private citizenship."

The public, some of which had been touting the President for a third term, responded with overwhelming approval of his decision. By taking so strong a position, McKinley had stated a basic American precept which needed affirmation at that moment. So much had happened in the previous five years that was outside the pattern of the American experience, that precedents were falling everywhere. Here, in his adherence to the unwritten rule of two terms for any one President, McKinley was reaffirming the American tradition when it needed such support. It was one of his strongest actions and finest moments.

# CHAPTER 13

# In Pursuit of Friendship

THE PAN-AMERICAN EXPOSITION of 1901 was organized to promote friendship and trade among the nations of the Americas, and in this regard it exactly represented the portion of his policy that President William McKinley wanted first to emphasize in this second term of office. He had been prevented from making his important policy addresses on the western trip by his wife's illness, but now she was well again and there was no reason that he should not pick up where he had left off.

The most urgent national and international affairs had been settled by the spring of 1901, and the President felt that this summer it would be possible to spend three months away from Washington's soggy heat. The change would be good for Ida, and for him too. He planned to spend much of this time in Canton, but the Pan-American Exposition was very important to him. So he was most pleased when he learned that the civic leaders of Buffalo had gotten together and planned that September 5 would be President's Day at the exposition.

On July 5, the presidential party left Washington for Canton. In Canton, McKinley walked out to talk to the gardener in the mornings and surveyed the small grounds of his house. He leaned over the fence to talk to passersby on the sidewalk. He was "just folks" and it was apparent that he was looking forward with eagerness to the day that he would pass on the cares of the presidency to another and return to this house to spend all his time.

During the summer he took a few trips by private railroad car, but they were brief excursions. Otherwise his travel was confined to drives into the countryside of Stark County with Ida, and his entertainment was talk with old friends, combined with music and card games.

As summer drew on, the plans for the President's stay at the Buffalo exposition were drawn up. Secretary Cortelyou read them and approved of all except one thing. There was to be a fireworks display, an excursion to Niagara Falls, a parade through the streets. All this was satisfactory. The President would stay at the home of John G. Milburn, the president of the exposition. This was fine, too. But on the schedule was a public reception at the Temple of Music on the fairgrounds, at which the President would appear and shake hands with all who chose to come through the reception line. Cortelyou violently objected to this plan because, he said, it threw the life of the President into jeopardy. The threats uttered by the anarchists against chiefs of state were not idle threats, as the murders of the past few years had shown.

McKinley refused to listen to his secretary. "I have no enemies. Why should I fear?" he asked.

Twice the public reception was taken off the program through the efforts of Cortelyou, and twice it was restored through the insistence of President McKinley. Cortelyou could do no more than caution the authorities at Buffalo to take every precaution. They were doing just that. The chief of police had already been in touch with his counterpart in Washington, and had asked for the advice of this experienced official in the handling of crowds around the President.

On September 5, when President McKinley appeared at the exposition, more than fifty thousand people crowded into the grounds to hear his speech on reciprocal trade. "Isolation is no longer possible or desirable," the President said. The United States must join the community of nations, and to do so it could not think of itself simply as a seller but must also be a buyer of goods from other countries.

The speech was most successful. Why should it not be? The President talked about the betterment of the American standard of living and of prosperity. That was the entire point of the address, and there was nothing unpleasant in it, unless one happened to be a manufacturer of goods in direct competition with cheaper and perhaps better goods from abroad; but among the crowd of 50,000 there were few such manufacturers. The President was greeted by cheer after cheer as he stopped for breath. The sustained cheering at the end of the speech amounted to a long, happy roar.

The President then toured the fair, lunched in the New York State Building, and held a small formal reception in the Government Building. He went to the Puerto Rican building to sip coffee for a moment, and toured the buildings and exhibits of the other foreign countries as an act of courtesy. That night he and Ida and their guests attended the fireworks display which they watched from the tower of the life saving station. The high point was a pyrotechnic portrait of the President, blazing away above the legend "Welcome to McKinley Chief of our Nation." Then, very tired, the President went back to the Milburn mansion and went to bed. The lights in the McKinley room were very quickly extinguished because it had been a long and tiring day.

The next morning the President put on his hard shirt, wing collar and starched cuffs, pin-striped trousers and morning coat, and set out on what he called the "restful day" of his visit. A special train took the presidential party to Niagara Falls. There McKinley spent the morning hiking and sight-seeing. Then he came back to the hotel, ate a large lunch, and relaxed with a cigar on the verandah. After a visit to the power house at the falls, it was time to board the train and return to Buffalo for the four o'clock reception. It would not be long; events had been added to the schedule so that now there were only about ten minutes allocated for the reception.

The reception committee had been at work all morning in the ornate Temple of Music to prepare for the event. It was decided to place the President at one corner of the dais and admit the greeters by only one doorway. They would walk along a wide aisle past the dais, and then could leave through a number of exits.

Three secret service agents were on duty that day with the President, and in addition a special guard had been provided at the reception. The danger to the President was recognized; and after a flippant remark about someone shooting the President was made, the Grand Marshal of the exposition became worried and increased the guard.

Before the President arrived, sight-seers had swarmed to the temple by the thousands. The line of those who hoped to pass by the dais and greet the President was very long, so long that only those who had arrived early, who had been standing for many hours, would have the slightest chance of speaking to him. Among these was a short, slender man, twenty-eight years old, with a clean-shaven face and sensitive eyes. He was Leon Czolgosz, once a hard-working mechanic in a Cleveland wire mill, son of Polish immigrants, a philosophical anarchist who did not belong to any group but who hated the American system of government. He had come to the Temple of Music this day with a .32-

caliber revolver in his pocket, determined to kill the President of the United States.

At four o'clock the President stepped from his carriage at the door of the Temple of Music and walked into the building in a burst of applause from the crowd. He crossed the auditorium and took his place. The reception began, and he started greeting people, smiling and shaking hands. The crowd was moving too slowly and Cortelyou went to tell the officials to hurry them along.

Five or six minutes after the reception started, Cortelyou looked at his watch, and the Grand Marshal of the exposition moved back to the doorway to be ready at a signal from the secretary to close the doors so that no more people could come through the line.

At this moment, Leon Czolgosz was just a few feet from the President. He had already passed the scrutiny of several Buffalo detectives, even though he had a handkerchief over his hand. This did not seem unusual, because it was an extremely hot day and people were constantly mopping their brows. Indeed, the President had three handkerchiefs on his person that day for just that purpose.

Then, as the President put out his hand to a short, slender man, the hand was thrust aside by a hard object, and two shots rang out. A thin cloud of smoke rose between the President and his assailant.

In a moment the vacant stare of the President was replaced by realization of what had happened. The vacant stare of the assassin was replaced by a grimace of pain as he was borne to the ground beneath the weight of police and others who wrested the gun from him and dragged him limp to the center of the hall.

"Don't let them hurt him," the President said, as he sank into a chair. He lifted a hand from his stomach and raised it to the shoulder of George Cortelyou who bent over him.

"My wife," he said in a whisper, "be careful, Cortelyou, how you tell her—oh, be careful."

Within a few moments the hall was empty. The assassin had been taken to another room by police, and an ambulance arrived to take the President to the emergency hospital on the exposition grounds, where he arrived at eighteen minutes after four.

The hospital was really little more than a first-aid station, but did have an emergency operating room. The President was taken there and undressed. As his underclothing was removed, a bullet fell out. The bullet fired at his ribs from the cheap revolver had simply bruised him; but the second shot, fired at his abdomen, had caused a serious wound.

A prominent Buffalo surgeon, Dr. Mathew D. Mann, and three assistant doctors began to operate. First, ether was given to the President, and then his abdomen was opened.

The surgeons found that the bullet had passed straight through the stomach. All they did was to clean out the peritoneal cavity and sew up the wounds. The bullet was not found, and no drainage canal was established. The President was then taken to the Milburn house.

All during the weekend the newspapers speculated on his condition. It was remembered that former-President Garfield had died of peritonitis. But by Monday the President's temperature had gone down, and the reporters working in a tent erected on the grounds of the Milburn mansion felt that the crisis was over. The second floor of the mansion had been turned into a temporary hospital, with doctors and nurses and members of the family in constant attendance.

The cabinet had assembled in Buffalo and Vice-President Theodore Roosevelt had been reached on an island in Lake Champlain, where he was on a typically vigorous outdoor vacation with his family. On Monday it was reported that the President had taken nourishment by tube, to avoid injury to his wounded stomach. A prominent New York physician said that his condition was satisfactory.

The cabinet began leaving Buffalo. On Tuesday doctors reported that if no complication arose, a quick convalescence might be expected. Secretary of State Hay arrived in Buffalo in a gloomy mood, but no one paid any attention to him. All were confident of the President's quick recovery, and Mrs. McKinley went out for a drive, feeling better than she had felt since that awful moment when she had gotten news of the shooting.

All the while that the doctors were reassuring the public, the bullet inside McKinley's abdomen was doing its evil work, and gangrene was coursing through his stomach, his pancreas, and one kidney, along the track where it had moved. The doctors paid no attention to the bullet. They refused the use of X-ray, although Charles Edison himself offered to bring X-ray machinery to the President's bedside. They acted in a thoroughly unprofessional and improper manner. By Thursday gangrene had done its work. By Friday, even as the doctors were dispersing and congratulating themselves, the President was dying.

In the late afternoon he spoke to the reassembled and frightened doctors. "It is useless, gentlemen," he said. "I think we ought to have prayer." Mrs. McKinley came in, and he said good-bye to her and to all the others. She remained by the bedside, holding his hand; he smiled up at her. Finally she left the room.

For two more hours the President's strong heart fought against the killing disease. But then his breathing became labored, and finally there was one last, labored gasp.

"The President," said the doctor in attendance, "is dead."

Then, for twelve hours, as a shocked and panic-stricken

nation wondered what had happened, the United States had no President. Teddy Roosevelt had been convinced by the doctors that McKinley was in no danger. He had gone to a camp high in the Adirondacks, where it took hours to reach him. A guide had found him high on top of a mountain. The telegrams the guide carried sent Roosevelt scurrying to Buffalo; but still it took more hours to cross the breadth of New York State once he reached transportation.

Roosevelt refused to see anyone except those speeding him along. A special train met him and carried him to Buffalo. He locked himself in a compartment and would not talk to the press. Almost as soon as he arrived, he took the oath of office, at the urging of the cabinet.

Then came five days of mourning, while McKinley's body was taken to Washington, and then to Canton for burial. It was a time of mourning, an awkward time, when the business of the nation could not be quite suspended, when the new President, mourning for the old, already had to be making plans for the future of the nation.

But it came to an end. McKinley was home in Canton, not resting beneath the roof of his Victorian house but beneath the ground in the graveyard, where he would be joined so soon by his wife.

# CHAPTER 14

# The Urge to Greatness

HAD McKINLEY not been cheated of three and a half years in the presidency, there is good reason to believe that he would have gone down in history as one of the great Presidents of the United States. The assassin, Leon Czolgosz, was quickly tried and quickly executed for his crime; yet the clock of history could not be turned back. Instead, the youthful Theodore Roosevelt set out to try to follow the McKinley program as he understood it.

It was impossible, of course for anyone but William Mc-Kinley to carry on a McKinley administration, but Roosevelt did try. The idea of imperialism and "manifest destiny" had not been McKinley's, although he had furthered them. Roosevelt continued in this path, advocating reciprocal trade and the assumption of America's strong place in the community of nations. America was to be in and out of that community for another forty years, and it was to be forgotten by many that the first American President to say that the United States could not remain in isolation was not Franklin Roosevelt, or Woodrow Wilson, or even Teddy Roosevelt, but William McKinley. In the footsteps of McKinley, Theodore Roosevelt's finest accomplishment was to call to public attention again and again the defects of the trust system in America. Under Roosevelt, action would be begun to put an end to the abuses of the trusts, but most of them would be carried out under the succeeding Taft administration. In the process it would be generally forgotten that the action originated in a policy declared by William McKinley.

What were McKinley's attributes as President and as citizen that might be remembered by Americans? One, certainly, was a totally blameless personal life and a high standard of personal honesty and integrity—one that was really beyond his time. It is a matter of record that the standards of honesty in public office in America improved steadily in the years that followed the Civil War, beginning at a very low point—Grant's administration. Even in such a period of improvement, McKinley's personal standards were noteworthy. McKinley also possessed a tact and political presence that enabled him to secure concessions from Congress where other men might not have been so successful. He did not always have a friendly Congress; he even fought with Senator Mark Hanna on some serious issues, but McKinley was always listened to with respect by Congress, and usually he got part of his way if not all of it.

McKinley missed one chance for greatness in history when he failed to draw the protective cloak of the flag over the people of the Philippines and the other possessions acquired in the Spanish-American War. He was cheated of greatness—the second chance—to put his international program into effect; for in his plans for reciprocal trade, which he understood and knew how to get, he might have advanced the entrance of the United States into the world arena by half a century. In McKinley's last address to the American people he stated the position that would have led him to this greatness.

"The period of exclusiveness is past," he said. "The expansion of our trade and commerce is the pressing problem. Commercial wars are unprofitable. A policy of good-will and friendly trade relations will prevent reprisals. Reciprocity treaties are in harmony with the spirit of the times; measures of retaliation are not." No nation, he said, could longer be indifferent to any other, and as they were brought together the nations must begin to adjust their differences in the court of arbitration. For as McKinley said, "Let us ever remember that our interest is in concord, not conflict; and that our real eminence rests in the victories of peace, not those of war." That was the legacy he wanted to leave the American people.

# Selected Bibliography

Grosvenor, Charles H. *William McKinley*. Washington, 1901.

Leech, Margaret K. *In the Days of McKinley*. New York: Harper, 1959.

Olcott, Charles S. *The Life of William McKinley*. 2 vols. Boston: Houghton Mifflin, 1916.

Porter, Robert P. *Life of William McKinley*. 4th ed. Cleveland: Hamilton Publishing Co., 1896.

Porter, Robert P. and James Boyle. *Life of William McKinley*. Cleveland: Hamilton Publishing Co., 1897.

Thayer, William R. *Life and Letters of John Hay*. 2 vols. New York: Houghton Mifflin, 1915.

# Index